The Touche R
Tax Guide for the
Self-Employed
1987/88

BILL PACKER, MA, FCA
National Tax Technical Director
Touche Ross

and

COLIN SANDY, ATII
Tax Manager
Touche Ross

PAPERMAC

First published 1985 by
PAPERMAC
a division of Macmillan Publishers Limited
4 Little Essex Street London WC2R 3LF
and Basingstoke

Associated companies in Auckland, Delhi, Dublin, Gaborone, Hamburg, Harare, Hong Kong, Johannesburg, Kuala Lumpur, Lagos, Manzini, Melbourne, Mexico City, Nairobi, New York, Singapore and Tokyo

Third edition published 1987

British Library Cataloguing in Publication Data

Packer, Bill
    A tax guide for the self-employed.——
    3rd ed.
    1. Self-employed——Taxation——Great Britain
    I. Title II. Sandy, Colin
    336.2'07   HJ4707

    ISBN 0–333–44963–0

Typeset by Wessex Typesetters
(Division of The Eastern Press)
Frome, Somerset
Printed in Great Britain by Richard Clay plc, Bungay, Suffolk

Contents

Preface to the 1987/88 Edition

For generations, people have been fired with enthusiasm to run their own business and in spite of the hard work and the financial risks involved to 'do their own thing'. It is not for nothing (as he may well have had cause to reflect somewhat ruefully in the years of exile) that Napoleon condemned the British as 'a nation of shopkeepers'.

It is perhaps ironic that income tax was introduced (only as a temporary tax!) into the United Kingdom at just about the same time as that remark was made, as taxation in all its forms represents one of the major challenges that the modern businessman or business-woman has to face.

This book sets out to identify and illuminate those areas of the tax legislation which need to be recognized by individuals in setting up and developing their own business and how the legislation can in many cases be turned to their advantage. Instead of approaching the subject by considering the legislation as it applies to specific aspects, the book follows the development of an imaginary business from its inception, through development and expansion, to its close. It also looks at the effects of going into partnership and of incorporation, as well as at some of the other issues that may be encountered, such as the obtaining of grants and the impact of employment law.

For simplicity the book sets out the authors' understanding of UK tax law and practice at 31 July 1987. In particular it takes into account the changes introduced in the two 1987 Finance Acts, especially those relating to value added tax (see 2.7) and inheritance tax on trusts (see 8.5).

Income tax is a tax on individuals and, except in a few particular instances, does not recognize any difference between the sexes. For simplicity throughout this book we have referred to the masculine gender but this should be read as including the feminine whenever appropriate.

While the book seeks to be as informative and comprehensive on these matters as possible, within the constraints of space, its application to any particular set of circumstances does require care and full appreciation of the relevant facts. In considering a specific situation relating to their affairs, readers should always seek competent professional advice.

The authors would like to record their thanks to Elaine Baker who provided much of the original inspiration for this book.

London 1987   WRP
                                                     CTS

1 So You Want to be Self-Employed

1.1 INTRODUCTION

This book follows the development of a business started by David Wiltshire, the problems he encounters and how these difficulties were overcome.

David Wiltshire, born 18 November 1939, has been employed by Widgetmasters PLC since he left school at the age of sixteen. His progress while with the firm has been steady, so that he is now a manager in charge of their technology development department. However, although advances in technology have been great, the company is not blessed with great marketing ability and so has been unable to make the best use of the development department's work. David has become increasingly frustrated with what he sees as a lack of commitment on the part of his colleagues within the company, and the corporate structure is such that he has been unable to progress and so influence the decisions regarding strategy and the company's longer-term future.

The alternatives open to him are to leave the company and either go to work for a competitor or set up his own business pursuing his work on the development of widgets in particular areas and marketing the product of this work himself.

In all that he does he is aware of the responsibilities he has to his family and their future. The family tree is set out below.

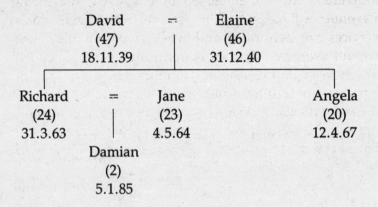

David and Elaine Wiltshire were married in 1960 and have two children, Richard and Angela. Richard has been married for three years to Jane and they have one son, Damian. Richard is undergoing training with Widgetmasters in the technology department but has shown an interest in joining his father in business. Angela is currently in her second year at university.

1.2 THE ADVANTAGES AND DISADVANTAGES OF BEING SELF-EMPLOYED

There are distinct advantages in being taxed on self-employed earnings under the rules of Schedule D, rather than on employed earnings under Schedule E, resulting from the method of payment of tax and the relief available for expenses incurred. In determining whether particular individuals are self-employed or employed, the Inland Revenue will consider the way in which individuals' services are performed and whether or not they have control over the way they perform their work. They will also have regard to whether an individual is occupied in a permanent position which would continue to exist even if that particular individual no longer filled the position. Thus the Revenue will look to see what arrangements have been made between the parties as to how the work will be controlled and performed.

A contract *for* services indicates self-employment and usually results in the person providing the service being paid to achieve a result and being left to his or her own devices in deciding how that result should be achieved. This would include the provision of equipment and the hiring of staff. A contract *of* service would be indicated where the individual's employer is in a position to instruct and dictate how and when the work to be performed should be undertaken. The distinction between the two, i.e. whether there is a master/servant relationship, was illustrated by Lord Denning as follows:

'A ship's master, a chauffeur, and a reporter on the staff of a newspaper are all employed under a contract of service; but a ship's pilot, a taxi-man and a newspaper contributor are employed under a contract for services.'

The Revenue will always try to argue that an individual is assessable under Schedule E rather than Schedule D because there are fewer deductions that can be obtained, due to the stricter requirements that need to be met, and the tax is paid significantly earlier.

The final decision must be based upon the facts of any particular case. Based on the decisions in a line of court cases, the Inland Revenue normally take the following factors into account in deciding if an individual should be assessed under Schedule D:

(1) The number of concurrent contracts held by the individual at any given time.
(2) The provision of tools and equipment, and the authority to hire and fire employees or subcontractors.
(3) Whether the manner of conducting the work is sufficiently autonomous.
(4) The degree of financial risk and whether the rewards are variable or fixed.
(5) The precise terms embodied in the agreement to conduct the work, i.e. is it demonstrably a contract of service or a contract for services?
(6) Control over day-to-day matters such as hours of work, review and accountability.

(7)   Whether the individual holds him/herself out as being in business on his/her own account, for example by undertaking work for other principals.

As has been said above, the opportunities for tax planning are greater under Schedule D than Schedule E because of the less stringent rules applying to expenses in respect of the former. For expenditure to be deductible under Schedule E, it must be incurred *wholly, exclusively and necessarily in the course of the performance of the duties of the employment*. This requirement is interpreted very strictly by the Revenue. For instance, a deduction of expenses incurred will not be allowed where the expense merely puts the employee in a position to do his duties; they will be allowed only if they are expended in the performance of those duties. (This aspect is dealt with in more detail in Chapter 4 of *The Touche Ross Tax Guide to Pay and Perks 1987/88* by Bill Packer and Elaine Baker; Papermac, 1987.) Under Schedule D, expenses are allowable if they can be said to be 'wholly and exclusively' for the purpose of the business. Thus the 'necessarily' requirement does not apply, which means that most expenses connected with the business, if only in part, will be allowed in calculating taxable profits.

Where losses are incurred there is also a great deal of flexibility in how these can be relieved against profits or other income of the trader and his or her spouse. In particular, where the business is in the first four years of its life any losses arising can be set against David's total income of the preceding three years. Losses are considered in more detail at 2.6. Other advantages are that when an individual disposes of business assets by way of gift or

sale to third persons, subject to certain conditions being
met, reliefs from capital gains tax and inheritance tax are
available. Again, these are considered in more detail later.

Certain disadvantages that David will face if he decides
to become self-employed are that:

(1) The pension contributions he has made to the company's pension scheme will help to support his
pension entitlement at retirement age and this is
looked at further in 1.4. Otherwise further provision
for his retirement and for his dependants is entirely
down to him.

(2) National insurance contributions will now be of the
Class 2 and Class 4 type (see 1.3). The former are flat
rate and the latter are related to profits, but the
important point here is that they do not entitle the
payer to unemployment benefit or to the additional
earnings-related pension element at present added to
a basic national insurance pension. Tax relief is
available on one-half of Class 4 national insurance
contributions.

(3) *There is nobody to provide holiday pay when a self-employed
individual decides to take a break. A week's holiday may be
a week's lost income (though not a week's lost expenses!).*

1.3 NATIONAL INSURANCE CONTRIBUTIONS – PAST AND FUTURE

The Social Security Acts provide for a range of benefits to
be paid to individuals in return for the payment of

contributions by them and, where appropriate, their employer towards the cost of providing these benefits. There are four classes of contribution:

Class 1 – primary: this applies to people in employment and is earnings related;
– secondary: this contribution is again earnings related and is paid by employers in respect of their employees.
Class 2 – this is a flat rate contribution payable weekly by people in self-employment.
Class 3 – this is a voluntary contribution paid by individuals not otherwise required to contribute who wish to enhance their entitlement to benefit.
Class 4 – this contribution is paid by those in self-employment and is profits related.

The rates in force for 1987/88 can be found in Appendix C. Note that contributions paid under Class 4 do not purchase any specific benefit entitlement at all but are merely seen by the Exchequer as a further contribution to be made to the general funding of benefits by those in self-employment.

David's company's pension scheme was not contracted out of the State scheme, so that reduced national insurance contributions were not paid in respect of earnings in excess of the lower earnings limit. Therefore, an additional earnings-related pension element has been purchased which will be added to the basic national insurance retirement pension.

The benefit that these payments have acquired are not lost merely by David becoming self-employed. Provided that he continues to pay full Class 2 contributions in each tax year he will secure a maximum basic national insurance retirement pension. Contributions may be credited automatically (instead of having to be paid) for periods of sickness or unemployment but it may be necessary to send sick notes to the local social security office or sign on at the unemployment benefit office to get the credits.

1.4 PAST CONTRIBUTIONS TO THE EMPLOYER'S PENSION SCHEME

If David leaves his employer to become self-employed he will have to look at his existing pension arrangements. If he already has a personal pension scheme in operation of the same kind as is used by self-employed individuals (see Chapter 5), he should have no difficulty in continuing this in his new situation. If, however, he was a member of an occupational pension scheme operated by his employer there are certain options open to him.

If he had remained with his employer he would have obtained the maximum pension benefit possible under his employer's scheme. Depending on the scheme rules, this would be based upon final remuneration and average benefits that he received multiplied by n and divided by 60 (or sometimes 80), where n equals the number of years of service with the employer. A lump sum of up to one and a half times final remuneration could have been taken on retirement in exchange for a reduction in the pension payable. Of course, had David's earnings increased substantially over the next eighteen years the loss of pension rights in cash terms could be substantial.

Normally pension schemes provide for the pension to be *frozen* in this type of situation. A 'frozen' pension is one preserved by the former employer's pension scheme and is normally linked to the employee's pay at the date the employment ceased. Concern has been expressed generally that this approach penalizes an employee where there are several job changes during his career. In its basic form this provides no protection against inflation. Therefore if pay levels were to rise substantially before retirement a pension linked to a salary some years earlier will purchase much less in real terms when it becomes payable. However, legislation now provides that, where the deferred pension option is taken, the benefit accruing after 1 January 1985 will be revalued each year in line with the retail prices index but subject to a maximum annual increase of 5%.

Also under an arrangement known as a 'Section 32 pension buy-out', a pension fund can allocate contributions relating to a particular employee to the purchase of a deferred annuity from an insurance company.

The leaver thereby receives the benefit of the whole amount of his own and his employer's contributions. On reaching retirement age the individual can take an 'open market option' to buy the best annuity available in the market, and with effect from 1 January 1986 this option became as of right irrespective of the rules laid down in the pension scheme.

The whole question of transferability of pension rights between different types of scheme is under active review by the government as part of its 'new deal' for employees' pensions and it is expected that new regulations on this aspect will be issued in the autumn of 1987.

1.5   PAYING TAX – HOW AND WHEN

Tax is collected in one of two ways: either by deduction at source or by way of an assessment issued by the Inspector of Taxes.

The most common example of tax being deducted at source is from employees. An employee will receive his or her weekly/monthly salary after tax and national insurance contributions have been deducted. An assessment may be made on an employee (which will show income and assessable benefits from employment and the tax deducted therefrom) after the end of the tax year if, for some reason, too much or too little tax has been paid despite the regular deductions made by the employer. This is the arrangement under which David would have paid his liabilities prior to leaving employment. If he becomes self-employed, accounts will need to be sent to the Inspector of Taxes showing details of income and expenditure for, usually, a year and the Inspector will then issue an assessment based on taxable profit for the relevant tax year, which will show him the amount of tax and Class 4 national insurance contributions he has to pay over.

Where the figures shown on the assessment are not agreed by him, a taxpayer has thirty days in which to appeal against it, stating his reasons and whether or not he wishes part, or all, of the tax charged to be postponed from collection until the figures have been agreed. The procedure for making an appeal or a request for postponement of the tax charged is covered in the notes which are always issued with a notice of assessment. Where an appeal is lodged on the grounds that the assessment is estimated and the Inspector of Taxes is awaiting accounts or other details, there should be as little further delay as possible in sending the information. The Inspector does have the right to take an appeal against a tax assessment before an independent body called the General Commissioners who, when the facts are put before them, have the power to determine, or confirm, the assessment in whatever amount they consider appropriate. This may lead to excessive tax being payable where the Inspector's figures cannot reasonably be disputed.

As will be seen from the above there is little cash flow advantage in being employed as the tax is deducted from salary. However, if David becomes self-employed he will normally pay the tax due in two equal instalments on 1 January during the year of assessment and on 1 July immediately following the end of the year of assessment. For the tax year 1987/88 tax is payable on 1 January 1988 and 1 July 1988 (remembering that the tax year commences on 6 April 1987 and ends on 5 April 1988).

If the assessment is issued too late to pay tax on these dates it will be due instead within thirty days after the date of the issue of the notice of assessment.

If there is tax to pay on an assessment then the notice will always state clearly the due date for payment of tax. An interest charge, currently at 8¼% per annum, accrues daily from what is called a reckonable date (which varies depending upon the circumstances) to the date payment of the tax is made. There is no point in delaying payments of tax after the due and payable date due to the risk of having to pay an interest charge. If an interest charge is incurred this is not deductible for any tax purpose.

If the situation is reversed and the Revenue owe a refund of tax there may be a non-taxable repayment supplement (in effect a form of interest) due as well. This is calculated at 8¼% per annum by reference to the date of payment of the tax. However, interest will not accrue before the end of the tax year in which the tax is paid.

The Revenue have adopted a practice whereby they do not collect arrears of tax if this has arisen due to some error on their part involving their failure to make proper and timely use of information provided to them relating to a taxpayer's income or personal circumstances. The proportion of arrears forgiven in this way depends on the taxpayer's gross income and ranges from all the tax being forgiven if his or her gross income is less than £8,500 to all the arrears being collected if the income exceeds £23,000.

Where a taxpayer is aged sixty-five or over or in receipt of national insurance retirement or widow's pension the above limits are increased by £2,500. These cases are not that common, and the Revenue looks at the circumstances very carefully before a case of 'official error' is admitted.

1.6 TAXABLE ELEMENT – SALARY v. PROFIT

SALARY

For employees the amount chargeable to tax for any tax year is the amount of the 'emoluments' for that year.

The statutory definition of 'emoluments' is 'all salaries, fees, wages, perquisites and profits whatsoever'. This covers a very wide area and *includes* the following:

Salaries	Pensions	Christmas boxes (in cash)
Fees	Bonuses	Pay during absence from work
Wages	Overtime pay	Payments for time spent travelling
Commission	Holiday pay	

Emoluments are effectively the benefits received by employees in return for which they work for their employer. They include benefits in kind as well, not just cash. However, certain benefits such as car and fuel scale benefits are not normally taxable where the employee receiving the benefit earns at a rate of less than £8,500 per annum (as defined – see 4.4.9) in any tax year.

PROFIT

The accounts profit is not necessarily the same figure as that which will be assessed to tax. The accounts profit has to be adjusted for tax purposes as not all the expenses shown in the accounts may be tax allowable. The primary rule is that expenses are allowable if they are incurred *wholly and exclusively* for the purposes of the business. It follows that where an expense was incurred partly for private purposes and partly for business purposes, the whole of the expenditure is not strictly allowable; usually, the Inspector is prepared to allow the business element if this can be apportioned on a reasonable basis.

Lists of the main allowable and disallowable items can be found in Appendices E and F respectively.

Worthy of a specific note is the tax treatment of *entertainment expenses*. These are not allowed except for staff entertainment within certain limits or the reasonable costs of entertainment of an *overseas* customer (as defined).

If expenses are incurred on the acquisition of a capital asset, a deduction may not be taken from trading profit. Assuming that the asset has a limited life span, its value to the business will gradually decline and this is anticipated by including in the accounts an amount for depreciation which is not, in itself, allowable for tax purposes. However, specific reliefs for capital expenditure, known as capital allowances, are given in taxing the trade and these are dealt with in more detail at 3.1.

2   The Early Years

David has decided that it would be more interesting for him to become self-employed as he considers that the potential advantages outweigh the disadvantages.

2.1   ADVISING THE REVENUE

As soon as the decision has been made to become self-employed the Revenue should be notified by the completion and submission of form 41G. Completion of this form notifies the local Inspector of Taxes of, among other things, the name under which the business is being carried on, the nature of the business, the date it started, if there are any partners and whether or not employees will be taken on. It also advises the Inspector of the name of the tax office to which the individual's last tax return was sent together with the reference number in that office. This is particularly important as it will enable a new Inspector to obtain any previous tax records so that David's affairs can be kept up to date. In David's case, he has given up a previous employment and should have received form P45

15

from his previous employer giving details of his pay and tax deductions to the date he left.

2.2   RECOVERY OF TAX PAID UNDER PAYE

The PAYE (Pay As You Earn) system operates on a 'cumulative' principle under which, as the tax year progresses, running totals are kept of the amount of emoluments received from the beginning of the tax year and of the tax deducted. Each time employers pay salary or wages they will deduct (or refund) the amount of tax which will keep the cumulative figure of tax deducted for each employee correct. Using this approach 1/12th of the reliefs and allowances available to the employee are given each month. Therefore where an employee leaves during the year to become self-employed there is a proportion of allowances that have not been utilized in arriving at the tax deducted to that date.

The accounts for the new business are likely to be prepared some time after the end of the tax year in which the employment ceases. It is not known whether the business will make a profit or a loss which can be apportioned to that fiscal year and which may be used in calculating the overall tax liability for the year. The Revenue therefore normally allow a tax repayment claim to be submitted in these circumstances on the basis that all allowances and reliefs due are allocated against the earnings to the date of leaving and any other known income for the year, and a tax repayment representing unused allowances at the taxpayer's top rate of tax is available. To the extent that there are surplus allowances these will be relieved against the profits eventually assessable in that tax year or, if these are still insufficient, they will be lost.

2.3 BOOKS AND RECORDS

The records that will need to be kept will depend upon the type and size of the business. It will be necessary to record all monetary transactions relating to the business and will include money received from customers for goods and services supplied and expenditure on purchases, wages and other items (see Appendices E and F for details of the types of expenditure that may be incurred). To assist in the preparation of a balance sheet a full record of drawings to meet private expenditure will be necessary as will details of cash injections.

Where there are stocks held for resale, either of completed goods or components, or partly completed work in progress, or significant quantities of goods of the kind which are consumed in the course of carrying on the business, at the end of an accounting period it will be necessary to value these because increases or decreases in their values have to be taken into account in determining profit. Stocks for resale and work in progress are usually valued at the lower of cost and realizable market value. Stores that are consumed in carrying on the business should be valued at cost.

Where customers do not pay for goods and services supplied immediately or where goods or services are supplied to David on credit, it will be necessary for him to keep records of the amounts owing to him (debtors) and amounts owing by him (creditors). This information is necessary if the true figure of profit earned in a particular accounting period is to be accurately reflected in the trading and the profit and loss accounts. This clearly makes good business sense because, notwithstanding that it is useful in preparing the accounts, it is essential that at any time David is fully aware of the money he owes and the money owed to him.

Various types of account books are available at stationery shops which have been specifically designed with particular trading ventures in mind. Account books are also available which have only been ruled into columns and which can be headed according to needs.

It is also necessary to keep adequate books and records for inspection by Customs and Excise in connection with VAT, and these are considered in more detail in 2.7.10.

Computers complete with business packages can also be acquired but, initially, this is not recommended unless it is clearly necessary to cope with the number of transactions involved, as the expenditure, although tax deductible under the capital allowances rules detailed below, so early in the life of a new business is a drain on working capital and this should obviously be avoided. In any case, care should be taken to see that any ready-made 'business package' offered with a computer is really apt to the requirements of the business. Professional advice may be particularly helpful here.

Remember that the Inspector can require that entries in accounts be supported, so all records, including bank statements, paying-in books, cheque stubs and supporting invoices or other vouchers, should be retained for at least six years.

To summarize, the detail that should be recorded is as follows:

(1) Sales.
(2) Business expenditure including purchases, rent, rates, lighting, heating, motor expenses, stationery, postage and telephone.
(3) Capital investment in the business.
(4) Drawings from business bank accounts or from petty cash for personal expenditure.
(5) The market value of any goods taken from the business for own or family use and not paid for at the full retail price. (Under tax law the trader is considered to be making a profit where he undertakes transactions with himself.)
(6) Amounts owed by customers (debtors).
(7) Amounts owed to suppliers (creditors).

2.4 TAXATION OF THE EARLY YEARS' PROFITS

It is important to determine when a trade, profession or vocation is set up or commenced. Prior to the trade commencing a certain amount of preliminary work, such as the construction of works or the installation of plant, may be necessary and early negotiations may have to be entered into for the purchase of materials and the sale or marketing of the business products created. Technically, a manufacturing trade could not have commenced until the business receives raw materials which can be used in the manufacturing process and thus become able to sell its products. In a retail or service business the trade can be said to have started when the operation is first open for business.

Where any expenditure which would normally be allowable is incurred in connection with the creation of a new business in the three years prior to the commencement of trading it may also be claimed as a deduction in the first year's tax assessment. (Somewhat similar rules apply in relation to VAT incurred on expenses prior to registration – see 2.7.7.) As has been explained it is much easier for a self-employed person to claim expenses in respect of his work than for an employee whose claim usually fails on the grounds that it is not a 'necessary' expense.

In the first three years of the life of the business there are special rules which decide how the profits arising from that business should be assessed to tax. The first year of assessment will tax the actual profits from the date the business started to the next 5 April, the end of the first *tax year* in which the business commenced. This will usually mean that the assessment is based on a proportion of the profits shown in the first accounts, computed on a time basis. In the second year of assessment the basis will be the actual profits of the first twelve months of trading from the date of commencement. However, if the first accounts are for a period of less than twelve months, the second and third years' assessments will also be made on a time basis (which would most probably mean a proportion of the profits from each of the first two sets of accounts). If the first accounts were prepared for a twelve-month period, the third year's assessment will be based on those accounts. This is called the previous year basis of assessment and will continue throughout the period of self-employment until the final years of the life of the business. Therefore as a general rule, the profits of an accounting period ending in the tax year 1986/87 will actually be taxed in 1987/88.

David will have the option to elect that all the first three years of assessment be made on the *actual* profits for those years but this will be advantageous only if the sums upon which he will be assessed are less than those charged using the normal basis. Therefore, as a general rule, the election will normally be made only if the profits of the second and third accounting periods are lower than those earned in the first year of trading. Claims for this treatment to be applied must be made within six years from the end of the third year of assessment affected.

Where an election is not advantageous the first twelve-month period will be the basis for the first three years' tax assessments, and it therefore follows that tax profits should be kept as low as possible. The net effect is that £1 of expenses can be relieved almost three times depending upon the accounting date finally decided upon.

To illustrate both the effect of the first three years' rules and the importance of choosing an advantageous accounting date a number of examples are set out below:

EXAMPLE 1

If David had commenced business on 6 October 1986
and the profits, as adjusted for tax purposes, for the
first year ended 5 October 1987 were £10,000, the
assessments would be as follows:

First year of assessment 1986/87
Period 6 October 1986 to 5 April 1987
   6/12 × £10,000   £5,000

Second year of assessment 1987/88
Period 6 October 1986 to 5 October 1987
(first 12 months)
   12/12 × £10,000   £10,000

Third year of assessment 1988/89
Based on profits arising in the trading year
ending in the previous year of assessment,
i.e. 1987/88; therefore year ended
5 October 1987   £10,000

Therefore profits have been assessed two and a half times.

Tax for 1988/89 is due as to one-half on 1 January 1989
and the balance on 1 July 1989. The delays from the end
of the accounting period to the dates tax is due are
approximately fifteen months and twenty-one months
respectively. The tax due in respect of the 1986/87 and
1987/88 tax years may be due earlier but this depends on
how early the accounts are submitted to the Revenue and
how quickly the Inspector issues the relevant assessments.

EXAMPLE 2

If David had commenced business on 1 May 1986 and his profits as adjusted for tax purposes for the first trading period of eight months ended 31 December 1986 and the year ended 31 December 1987 were £15,000 and £12,000 respectively, the assessments would be as follows:

	£
First year of assessment 1986/87	
Periods 1 May to 31 December 1986	15,000
1 January to 5 April 1987	
3/12 × £12,000	3,000
	£18,000

	£
Second year of assessment 1987/88	
Profits of first 12 months of trading	
Periods 1 May to 31 December 1986 (8 months)	15,000
1 January to 30 April 1987 (4 months)	
4/12 × £12,000	4,000
	£19,000

	£
Third year of assessment 1988/89	
Based on profits arising in the trading year ending in the previous year of assessment, i.e. 1987/88; therefore year ended 31 December 1987	**£12,000**

Therefore total profits of £27,000 for the twenty-month period have been assessed 1.8 times.

Again, tax for 1988/89 is due as to one-half on 1 January 1989 and the balance on 1 July 1989. The delays from the end of the accounting period to the dates tax is due are twelve months and eighteen months respectively. Again, the tax due for 1986/87 and 1987/88 may be due earlier as described above.

EXAMPLE 3

If David had commenced business on 1 December 1986 and his profits as adjusted for tax purposes were £17,000 for the seventeen months ended 30 April 1988 the assessments would be as follows:

First year of assessment 1986/87
Period 1 December 1986 to 5 April 1987
   4/17 × £17,000   £4,000

Second year of assessment 1987/88
Period 1 December 1986 to 30 November 1987
   12/17 × £17,000   £12,000

Third year of assessment 1988/89
Based on profits of preceding year   £12,000

Therefore total profits for the period have been assessed 1.65 times.

As before, tax for 1988/89 is due as to one-half on 1 January 1989 and the balance on 1 July 1989. The delays from the end of the accounting period to the dates tax is due are twenty months and twenty-six months respectively. The tax due in respect of the 1986/87 and 1987/88 tax years may be due earlier as described above.

In the examples given above it can be seen that the use of a 30 April year end not only results in a reduced multiplier effect on the initial profits realized by the business but also gives the opportunity to maximize the delay before tax is payable and thus to give the business a cash flow advantage. For simplicity profits have been apportioned in months, but days should be used where the amounts involved are substantial and a decision as to whether to elect for 'actual' for the first three years may be critical.

An example of where a taxpayer has decided that his first three years of trading should be assessed on a current year basis is described below.

EXAMPLE 4

Suppose David commenced business on 1 January 1986 and his profits, adjusted for tax purposes, in the years ended 31 December 1986, 1987 and 1988 were £12,000, £6,000 and £9,000. A decision whether to follow the normal rules or elect to be assessed on the actual profits in each tax year would be reached as follows:

Original assessments on normal basis

First year of assessment 1985/86   £
Period 1 January 1986 to 5 April 1986
   3/12 × £12,000   3,000

		£
Second year of assessment 1986/87		
Period 1 January to 31 December 1986		
12/12 × £12,000		12,000
Third year of assessment 1987/88		
Preceding year to 31 December 1986		12,000
		£27,000

After election

	£	£
1985/86		
As before		3,000
1986/87		
Actual 6 April 1986 to 5 April 1987		
Period 6 April to 31 December 1986		
9/12 × £12,000	9,000	
Period 1 January to 5 April 1987		
3/12 × £6,000	1,500	
		10,500
1987/88		
Actual 6 April 1987 to 5 April 1988		
Period 6 April to 31 December 1987		
9/12 × £6,000	4,500	
Period 1 January to 5 April 1988		
3/12 × £9,000	2,250	
		6,750
		£20,250

In each case the assessment for 1988/89 will be on the preceding year basis as usual, i.e. £6,000.

Therefore, in these circumstances, David would elect for the current year basis to apply for the first three years and by doing so would save tax as the corresponding assessments will be reduced by a total of £6,750.

As a general rule, where profits are rising an election will not be beneficial whereas where they are declining it will be. However, the calculations should always be done, by reference to days as mentioned above, so as to be quite sure of the position.

2.5 CHOOSING THE ACCOUNTING DATE

When commencing a new business most people will choose either to prepare a set of accounts for twelve months from the date that they commence business, whenever that may be, or to end an accounting period at the end of the tax year, i.e. 5 April. One advantage of preparing a first set of accounts which lasts for twelve months is that the first three years' tax assessments can be settled early but this is not necessarily an advantage worth taking. Advice should always be taken before an accounting date is chosen as there may be an advantage in choosing a particular date depending upon the line of business being carried on. However, as already seen, it is commonly most advantageous to choose a date that is early in the tax year, e.g. 30 April. This is because the choice of an accounting date is not so much a way of saving tax but of deferring payment of that tax and this is brought about due to the preceding year basis of assessment applicable to unincorporated businesses.

2.6 MAKING A LOSS

Where a loss arises in the first four years of assessment after the trade commences, an individual can offset it against the income of the three years of assessment preceding the year in which the loss is incurred, relieving the earliest year first. A loss incurred in an earlier year of assessment is relieved in priority to a loss incurred in a later year of assessment. A claim for this relief must be made in writing within two years after the end of the year of assessment in which the loss is sustained.

EXAMPLE 5

If David had commenced trading on 1 January 1986 with the results shown, the position would be as follows:

	Earnings £	Trading profit/(loss) £
1982/83	4,000	
1983/84	5,000	
1984/85	6,000	
1985/86		(6,000)
1986/87		(4,000)
1987/88		3,000

(It is assumed that neither David nor his wife has any other income in the years concerned.)

With such a claim the loss of £6,000 incurred in 1985/86 is allowed first against the income of 1982/83 and the balance against that for 1983/84. The loss of £4,000 incurred in 1986/87 is allowed first against the balance of £3,000 available in 1983/84 and the final £1,000 of loss is offset against the earnings of £6,000 in 1984/85. Tax will be repaid together with repayment supplement at a rate, currently, of 8¼% per annum. However, always be aware that personal allowances may be irretrievably lost. In the example above it can be seen that all income for 1982/83 and 1983/84 has been extinguished, therefore personal allowances have not been utilized. In certain situations it may be preferable not to claim the loss but for it to be carried forward instead against later years' profits. Remember that personal allowances cannot be carried forward.

Generally it is possible to set a trading loss against other income received in the particular year of assessment or in the following year of assessment provided that the trade is still being carried on in a commercial way with the view to the realization of profit. Again, a claim has to be made within two years of the end of the year of assessment in question and the loss must be set off against other earned income followed by unearned income. Where the person making the loss extinguishes his or her other income, any balance of loss available can be set against the spouse's earned income and, if there is still a balance left, the spouse's unearned income, unless a claim is made to the contrary. The repayment of tax follows in the usual way.

Losses can also be carried forward to be set against subsequent years' profits. Certainly, if relief is claimed under the provisions mentioned above, an immediate benefit of tax repayment, together with repayment supplement, is realized, but it may be more beneficial to carry all losses forward to a later year to be set against future profits from the same trade. Even where loss relief is claimed, either by setting off the loss against other income in the year or by carrying it back if it was incurred in the first few years of trading, there may still be a balance and this may be carried forward. A loss can be carried forward indefinitely until it is completely used up provided only that the same trade is still being carried on.

Any loss arising in connection with a trade can be augmented by capital allowances available in connection with certain expenditure incurred on capital assets, e.g. plant or machinery, which are used for the purposes of the trade. Capital allowances are dealt with in Chapter 3.

2.7   VALUE ADDED TAX

VAT was introduced into the UK with effect from 1 April 1973 as an indirect tax on final consumer expenditure. The Commissioners of Customs and Excise administer VAT through a computer centre at Southend and a network of local VAT offices situated in major towns. The computer centre deals with tax returns and receives payments of VAT from, and makes repayments of VAT overpaid to, registered persons. The local VAT office deals with the actual registration and deregistration of traders and also arranges control visits to ensure that the VAT rules are being correctly applied by traders.

VAT is charged on the supply of goods and services in the UK where the supply is a *taxable supply* made by a *taxable person* in the course or furtherance of a *business* carried on by him. Tax is charged by the taxable person making the supply and he is required to pay the amounts charged over to Customs on a quarterly basis. This tax is known as *output tax*.

VAT is also charged when goods are imported into the UK. The importer pays over any tax due direct to Customs (together with any import duties arising at the same time) but can then reclaim this as *input tax* as described in 2.7.1.

2.7.1 Taxable persons

Taxable persons effectively act as unpaid tax collectors for Customs and Excise.

To ensure that business entities do not themselves pay VAT, taxable persons can obtain a credit for VAT which they have borne (known as *input tax*) against VAT which is due from them. Where the VAT paid exceeds that due, Customs will make a direct repayment. Input tax normally consists of tax charged on goods and services supplied by other taxable persons and tax paid on goods imported.

Certain items of input tax are *not deductible*, notably that arising on *business entertaining*, in the same way and with the same exceptions as for income tax (see 1.6), and on the purchase of *motor cars* for business use.

There may also be some restriction of input tax where a part of the supplies made by the business is *exempt* from VAT (see 2.7.4).

2.7.2   Taxable supplies

As has been stated, VAT is charged on supplies of goods and services made in the UK. *Supply* is a broad term which can be said to comprise the passing of possession of goods or the provision of services in the course of carrying on a business. A supply of goods may encompass the transferring of ownership of goods, i.e. on a sale, or submitting another person's goods to some treatment or process, or supplying power, heat, refrigeration or ventilation, or the granting of a freehold interest in land or a lease for a term capable of exceeding 21 years. A supply of services may be the work of a professional adviser or can apply to the transfer of the possession, but not the ownership, of goods, for example by the hire, lease, rental or loan of an asset.

Goods or services taken from the business for private or other non-business purposes are treated as if they were supplies made by the business, and output tax needs to be accounted for on the market value of such notional supplies.

In particular, with effect from 6 April 1987, where a registered trader uses petrol (or other fuel) which is provided from business resources for private journeys, *either by himself or by his employees*, the trader is required to account for output tax on a notional supply according to a scale depending on the size of the engine. This is based on the petrol scale used by the Inland Revenue for calculating the benefit in kind for income tax purposes on petrol supplied to certain employees using company cars for private purposes. The scale laid down is as follows:

Cylinder capacity	Notional quarterly output (including VAT)	VAT at 15%
Up to 1,400cc	£120	£15.65
1,401–2,000cc	£150	£19.56
Over 2,000cc	£225	£29.34

Where the business mileage exceeds 4,500 a quarter, the scale charge is reduced by a half.

2.7.3 Business

This term is much broader than usually applies for income tax purposes and includes any occupation or function actively pursued with a reasonable level of continuity regardless of whether or not a profit motive exists, unless it can be shown that the activity is carried on solely for pleasure or social enjoyment. The term does specifically include:

(1) The carrying on of a trade, profession or vocation including a hobby organized in a business-like fashion.
(2) The provision of facilities by clubs to members.
(3) The admission of people to premises for a consideration.

This definition is far from exhaustive and any particular situation will have to be decided on its own facts.

Once an activity has been classified as a business any supply made while it is being pursued is likely to be made in the course or furtherance of that business. Unlike income tax no distinction is made between revenue and capital. The result of this is that a sale of surplus plant is regarded as much a supply as the sale of trading stock would be. There is also no distinction between trading and investment income, so rental income and interest received in connection with the business can be regarded as the consideration received for a supply made in the course or furtherance of the business.

2.7.4 Exempt supplies

Certain supplies of goods or services are exempt from VAT, in particular the use of land, and the provision of insurance and finance, health and education. A person making exempt supplies only is not a taxable person and cannot be registered. No tax is charged on such a supply but where exempt supplies are made by a business as well as taxable supplies the effect is that not all the input tax credit may be reclaimed, only that proportion relating to its taxable supplies.

As indicated in 2.7.1, some restriction of input tax may be applicable where a business has a mixture of taxable (including zero rated (see 2.7.5)) and exempt supplies; such a business is said to be *partly exempt* from VAT. Many businesses are regularly in this situation, for example those in the property, construction or financial services fields. However, many other businesses, normally fully taxable, could find themselves treated as partly exempt by reason of the sale of a property or the receipt of rent or of bank deposit interest.

A fundamental principle of VAT is that input tax attributable to exempt outputs should not be recoverable. Where there is a mixture of taxable and exempt outputs, the input tax borne by the business should be apportioned between those categories of output on a reasonable basis. How this apportionment is made is a matter for agreement between the trader and Customs. Until recently many arrangements have been agreed based on a specific attribution of inputs to taxable and exempt outputs where it was possible to do this, with an allocation of the remaining deductible input tax pro rata between taxable and exempt outputs. Frequently, the whole of the input tax was allocated in this way in the interests of simplicity and convenience. There were also rules that enabled exempt outputs to be ignored if they were sufficiently small or incidental in relation to the business.

With effect from 1 April 1987, the existing rules relating to partial exemption have been substantially modified so as to require a more specific attribution of inputs to taxable and exempt outputs. The 'de minimus' and 'incidental' rules have also been amended.

The upshot of these changes is that any business with some, even small, exempt outputs may find that its ability to recover input tax is reduced. It may therefore need to take professional advice as to any arrangements that it can make to contain this reduction.

2.7.5 Tax rates

Taxable supplies may be charged to tax either at the zero rate or at a standard rate. Although the zero rate means that no tax is charged on a supply, it is taken into account in determining whether a trader is a taxable person and it does not restrict input tax credits unlike exempt supplies described in 2.7.4. The more important types of supply taxed at the zero rate are supplies of food, books, newspapers, news services, fuel and power, the export of goods and certain services, transport and young children's clothing and footwear. There has been some comment regarding the wide range of goods and services covered by the zero rating provisions and it is anticipated that a number of those mentioned above will, at some time in the future, be treated as normal taxable supplies charged at the standard rate (see 2.7.6) or possibly at a reduced rate, so that the UK's VAT regime moves more closely into line with those of our EC partners.

It will be remembered that certain supplies, previously zero rated, have been recently made subject to tax at the standard rate, notably the alteration of buildings and the sale of hot take-away foods in 1984 and the supply of newspaper advertising in 1985.

2.7.6   The standard rate

There is only one standard rate of tax applied in the UK at present, namely 15% on the tax exclusive value of goods or services supplied. Where the tax is calculated as inclusive this is equivalent to a 'VAT fraction' of 3/23. Any supply which is not charged to tax at the zero rate or which is not exempt from VAT *must* be charged to tax at the standard rate.

2.7.7   Registration

Where a trader makes taxable supplies, and his or her taxable turnover exceeds £21,300 in four consecutive quarters, or turnover for a particular quarter exceeds £7,250, he or she must register with Customs for VAT purposes. These turnover limits apply after 17 March 1987. Traders who are liable to be registered under either of these provisions must inform Customs not later than 30 days after the end of the quarter in which their taxable turnover exceeded the statutory limits. They are then registered with effect from the twenty-first day of the new quarter or on a mutually agreeable date. The quarter ends for VAT accounting purposes will be determined by the nature of the business and do not necessarily coincide with the accounting period of the business.

Where traders would be liable to be registered under the above rules, they may obtain Customs agreement that they need not be registered if they meet one or other of the following conditions:

(1)   *Fluctuating turnover*. Where the turnover exceeds the limit for one quarter but the turnover for that quarter and the next three quarters is not expected to exceed the limit for a full year. Thus, if David's turnover for the quarter ended 30 September 1987 was £8,000 he will not be required to be registered if he can satisfy Customs that his turnover for the period 1 October 1986 to 30 June 1987 will not exceed £21,300 minus £8,000, i.e. £13,300.

(2) *Zero rated turnover*. Where turnover comprises only
    zero-rated supplies, such as food, and the trader is
    willing to forgo his right to reclaim input tax.

Where, at any time, a trader considers that his future
taxable turnover for a one-year period is likely to exceed
the four-quarter limit of £21,300 it is his duty to notify
Customs no later than the beginning of that period; he
will then be registered with effect from that date or
some other mutually agreeable earlier date. This rule will
certainly apply where a trader, starting a new business,
has expectations that he or she will do well and that the
business will expand rapidly.

It is possible for a trader whose taxable turnover is less
than the limits mentioned above to apply for *discretionary*
registration. Customs have a great deal of flexibility as to
whether or not they will accept such an application and
can impose conditions if they so choose. Discretionary
registration is not granted as a matter of course. Customs
must be satisfied that the business is of a reasonably
substantial scale and that the income from it is an important
part of the trader's livelihood. It must also be demonstrated
to them that supplies are taking place with a degree of
frequency and there must be a compelling business need,
such as the trader being otherwise at a serious trading
disadvantage, were registration to be denied. In practice,
this would mean that the trader would have to show that
if unregistered he would incur a substantial amount of
irrecoverable input tax.

However, the Customs attitude to discretionary registration is hardening and they will not, for example, allow

discretionary registration for traders such as hobby farmers or market gardeners even where there is an expectation that within a few years the turnover limits will be exceeded. Their approach is also to allow registration in such cases from a 'current' date. However, subject to certain tests being satisfied, Customs will allow a claim for input tax incurred prior to the date of registration, in the case of goods where these have not already been 'consumed' in the business, and in the case of services, up to six months before registration.

Where it is intended that taxable supplies will be made some time in the future at a level which will exceed the turnover limits mentioned above, Customs may allow what is called *intending trader* registration.

As a general rule, and provided the traders' expectations are not unreasonable, it must be advantageous to apply for VAT registration immediately where taxable supplies are to be made so that input tax incurred initially may be recovered. Again, Customs do have powers to impose conditions and it is likely that they will revoke registration where the trader's expectations are not met within a reasonable period. This may result in the loss of relief for VAT already incurred and the recovery of any such tax already paid.

Finally it must be emphasized again that the onus is on the trader to notify Customs that he or she is liable to be registered for VAT. While there may be some scope for controlling the situation as the turnover threshold is approached, once over the limit, as defined earlier, the trader *must* advise Customs of the position. Failure to register at the proper time can lead to the trader not only

being required to pay over arrears of output tax but also
being charged penalties.

2.7.8   Tax invoices

Except as described below, a tax invoice must be issued
not later than thirty days after the time when a taxable
supply of goods or services is made by registered taxable
persons. The original tax invoice is sent to customers and
is their evidence that they have paid input tax. A copy
should be kept by the trader to support his calculation of
output tax. Where the supplies are zero-rated or if the
customer is not a taxable person a tax invoice need not be
issued.

A tax invoice must contain the following information:

(1)   An identifying number.
(2)   The date of supply.
(3)   The supplier's name, address and registration
      number.
(4)   The customer's name and address.
(5)   The type of supply made, e.g. sale, hire purchase,
      loan, exchange, hire.
(6)   A description which identifies the goods or services
      supplied.
(7)   The value (expressed in sterling) and rate of tax for
      each supply.
(8)   The rate of any cash discount offered.
(9)   The amount of tax payable (expressed in sterling).

Where the registered person is a retailer, a tax invoice
need not be provided unless a customer who is a taxable

person requests it. In this situation, and provided the tax inclusive consideration does not exceed £50, generally a less detailed invoice will suffice which need contain only the information under (2), (3), (6) and (7) above. However, the invoice must include only those items subject to the same rate of tax.

The time of supply (known as the *tax point*) is the date on which goods or services are treated as being supplied. Goods are treated as supplied when they are delivered, collected or made available to a customer and services are treated as supplied when they are performed.

As these rules may be somewhat difficult to apply in practice, the date of the tax invoice issued in connection with the supply is normally taken as the tax point, *provided that this is not later than 14 days after the basic tax point already defined*. In any case, where *payment* is received earlier than these times, the date of payment is taken as the tax point.

There are special rules covering more complex supplies such as goods on sale or return, continuous supplies (e.g. electricity), periodical payments and sales under hire purchase.

In the 1985 Finance Act, new and more stringent penalties were introduced to deal with a variety of offences against the VAT regulations; in particular these concern failure to put in accurate VAT returns on time. While these penalty provisions are being introduced in stages (the first of these to deal with delayed returns being in operation since October 1986), it is vital that every registered trader reviews his or her accounting arrangements *now* to make sure that he or she can meet these requirements without possible liability to penalties.

2.7.9   Accounting for VAT

A registered trader is normally required to account for VAT quarterly by reference to a quarterly cycle fixed at the time of registration (see 2.7.7). The trader is automatically sent a return form by the Customs computer centre in Southend towards the end of each quarter and this is then required to be returned with any payment due so as to be *received* in Southend by the end of the month following the quarter concerned. A few days' extra time may be obtained where payment is made by bank giro transfer. The amount of VAT due with each return is the output tax arising for the quarter (i.e. on tax invoices issued during the quarter), less the amount of deductible input tax (see 2.7.1) charged to the trader in the same period. Where the amount of input tax charged in the quarter exceeds the corresponding output tax the excess is repaid by Customs, normally within ten days of their receiving the return.

Where a trader is regularly claiming VAT refunds because all or most of his outputs are zero rated, he may make monthly returns and be repaid accordingly.

It will be appreciated that on this basis traders may be required to account for output tax to Customs before it has been paid to them by their customers; bad debt relief is generally only available where the customer becomes formally insolvent.

This does impose some additional cash flow strain on smaller businesses; to alleviate this Customs proposes to introduce optional accounting arrangements for business with an annual turnover of £250,000 or less, as follows:

(1) From October 1987 such businesses will be able to make VAT returns and account for the tax on a *cash basis*, i.e. on the VAT element of cash received from customers less the VAT element of payments made to suppliers. This will provide an automatic relief for bad debts.
(2) From the summer of 1988 such businesses will also be able to complete returns on an annual basis. It is likely that they will be required to make nine monthly payments to Customs by direct debit during the year; they will then make a return for the whole year within two months of its end and pay over or reclaim any balance.

Special VAT accounting arrangements are also available to retailers and to dealers in certain categories of second-hand goods.

2.7.10 Books, records and control visits

Every taxable person must keep records of all business operations that may affect the VAT payable or reclaimable. These would include:

(1) Every supply of goods or services received on which VAT is charged by suppliers.
(2) Every importation or removal from a bonded ware-house.
(3) All supplies made by the business (including any zero-rated or exempt supplies).

(4)   Any goods exported.
(5)   Any gifts or loan of goods.
(6)   Any taxable supplies for private use.
(7)   Any goods acquired or produced in the course of the business put to a private or other non-business use.

Any adjustments to these records must also be noted such as:

(a)   corrections to accounts;
(b)   amended tax invoices;
(c)   any credits allowed or received.

These records must be retained for at least six years together with other normal business records, such as purchase and sales books and bank statements, mentioned at 2.3 above.

As part of their overall control of VAT, at intervals of between one and three years Customs officers may visit the business premises to check records and accounts with a view to ensuring that the tax is being correctly calculated and accounted for in both the past and the future. Where cash transactions are involved, gross profit and mark-up calculations may be made and the results compared with similar businesses.

2.8   GOVERNMENT ASSISTANCE

A measure of assistance may be forthcoming from a number of government agencies provided their specific requirements are met.

Some measures apply throughout the country, but others apply only in designated assisted areas to encourage businesses to move to them or expand or modernize an existing operation there, primarily to create or safeguard employment. Broadly, these assisted areas comprise:

• The whole of Northern Ireland.
• Parts of the west and centre of Scotland.
• Parts of the north and south of Wales.
• In England, parts of the North-east (especially around Newcastle-upon-Tyne, Hull and Sheffield), the North-west (especially around Liverpool), the West Midlands (around Birmingham), and the far South-west.

They are graded into development areas and intermediate areas. The basis on which aid is granted and the localities to which it is directed are both periodically reviewed, and up-to-date information can be obtained from the Department of Trade and Industry.

Assistance throughout the country would include the following:

(1) Aid for specific projects, which may be granted for major and innovative manufacturing ventures that would be in the national interest but would not be undertaken without it. Such aid is negotiable, and besides grants towards capital expenditure may include subsidies towards training, development, marketing and other costs.

(2) In localities suffering from special restructuring pro-
     blems because of the closure or rationalization of
     coal and steel, shipbuilding or textile industries, the
     European Regional Development Fund can make grants
     to stimulate new businesses. These grants are add-
     itional to loans that may be available from the Euro-
     pean Coal and Steel Community loans.
(3) Numerous grants and subsidies are available in the
     agricultural, horticultural, fishing and forestry sectors.
(4) Grants are available towards *mineral exploration costs*
     in Great Britain or the UK sector of the Continental
     Shelf.
(5) The English, Scottish and Welsh Tourist Boards admin-
     ister schemes to encourage the *development of tourism*,
     whereby grants (and occasionally loans) are made
     towards capital costs.
(6) Several schemes are designed to support *employment
     creation projects* and to provide training, especially for
     young workers.

On a regional basis investment in machinery, equipment
and buildings used by manufacturing industries in the
development areas (not the intermediate areas) are eligible
for regional development grants. Specified repair activities,
scrap and waste material processing, scientific research,
staff training relating to such industries, and a range of
business service activities also qualify for these grants.
Broadly, projects must create jobs in the development
areas, or create or expand productive capacity, to qualify
for grants.

Grant is calculated in one of two ways: as a capital grant or as a job grant. Payment is automatically made at the higher rate. Capital grant is a fixed 15% of the approved amount of capital expenditure subject to a grant per job limit of £10,000 (which is not normally applied to firms with less than 200 employees unless project expenditure exceeds £500,000). Job grant is £3,000 for each net job created. However, for manufacturing projects the total job grant may not exceed 40% of initial investment irrespective of the number of jobs created.

Regional development grants are not taxable, and unlike other government grants, they do not have to be deducted from cost when calculating tax allowances on the assets concerned.

Projects in both the development and the intermediate areas, in all sectors of industry and commerce, may be aided through regional selective assistance under section 7 of the Industrial Development Act 1982. As in the case of national selective assistance, an assisted project must be in the national interest; for example, it must contribute to the national economy by increasing output, introducing new technology, creating new employment or safeguarding existing employment in the assisted areas. Moreover, the project must be one that is likely to be economically viable but which would not take place without assistance. The greater part of the project's cost must be met from private sector sources.

The amount and terms of assistance given are negotiated individually, but the normal form is a grant, principally towards capital costs, payable in annual instalments. Up to 80% of training costs may also be subsidized. Regional selective assistance is not available if the project concerned has qualified for national selective assistance.

2.8.1   Enterprise Zones

These are relatively small areas in various parts of the UK which have been designated for special relief from certain tax, planning and administrative burdens in an effort to promote them as centres of enterprise. Currently there are seventeen such zones in England, at Corby, Dudley, Glanford, Hartlepool, Isle of Dogs, Middlesbrough, North East Lancashire, North West Kent, Rotherham, Salford, Scunthorpe, Speke, Telford, Tyneside, Wakefield, Wellingborough and Workington; three in Wales, at Delyn, Milford Haven and Lower Swansea Valley; three in Scotland, at Clydebank, Invergordon and Tayside; and two in Northern Ireland, at Belfast and Londonderry.

The following benefits are available, for a ten-year period from the date of designation of each zone, to industrial and commercial enterprises (both new and existing) in the zones:

(1) Exemption from general rates on commercial and industrial property.
(2) 100% tax allowances on investment in industrial and commercial buildings of all kinds. This therefore goes much further than the limited relief for industrial buildings described in 3.4.
(3) Exemption from industrial training levies.
(4) Simplified planning arrangements.
(5) Speeding up of Customs facilities.

(6)   Reduced requirements to provide statistical information to the authorities.

2.8.2   Development Agencies

The Scottish and Welsh Development Agencies, the Northern Ireland Industrial Development Board and associated bodies can provide discretionary loans, and may sometimes subscribe equity capital for appropriate companies.

The Department of Trade and Industry operates a Small Firms Service to improve the availability of information and business advice to small firms. More specialized advisory services are also available for small businesses on such matters as manufacturing, quality control, design, energy conservation and computerization.

2.8.3   Local Enterprise Agencies

These are advisory organizations, usually funded by large companies with local authority support, that aim to provide business advice and counselling to small firms. Some agencies also provide training workshops and organize exhibitions and seminars on business topics.

2.8.4   Enterprise Allowance scheme

The Manpower Services Commission operates a scheme which sets out to assist unemployed people who wish to start their own business. The scheme is designed to assist people who would otherwise be deterred by paying an Enterprise Allowance of £40 per week for up to fifty-two weeks to supplement business receipts whilst they are becoming established, provided that recipients contribute at least £1,000 of capital from their own resources. The scheme also provides access to free business counselling.

The allowance is subject to tax as part of the claimant's trading profits. However, payments received after 18 March 1986 will be liable to tax and national insurance contributions only once and will not be subject to the multiple charge on profits which normally applies in the opening years of a business (see 2.4).

2.8.5 'Burdens on business'

On a somewhat different note, there has been mounting pressure on the Government to simplify and reduce the bureaucracy and compliance requirements which at present are imposed on business, especially small business, over a wide range of their activities. In this connection, in July 1985 and May 1986 the Government issued White Papers setting out proposals for reducing these requirements and a number of these have been put into effect.

3 Capital Expenditure and Allowances

David Wiltshire has set up his business but he now requires machinery and premises in which to run it.

3.1 CAPITAL EXPENDITURE

Where expenses are incurred in the acquisition of capital assets the expense cannot be deducted direct in arriving at trading profit. As mentioned above, in computing taxable profits amounts charged as depreciation in the accounts are added back. The depreciation element in the accounts assumes that the asset has a limited life span and that its value to the business will gradually decline. This concept is recognized by the legislators and they have therefore introduced allowances in respect of certain capital expenditure which are available subject to certain conditions being met and which take the form of a standardized depreciation.

The main types of capital expenditure that will attract an allowance are:

• Machinery and plant.

- Industrial buildings.
- Agricultural buildings.
- Mines, oil and mineral deposits.
- Dredging.
- Scientific research.
- Patents.
- Knowhow.

The first three of these categories (being the most common) are dealt with in detail below.

It is possible that a particular item of capital expenditure falls into more than one category and it is normally possible to claim allowances in the most advantageous way, but there are special provisions which sometimes restrict this choice. In general the granting of allowances falls into three stages:

(1) An *initial or first-year allowance* of a substantial percentage of the capital expenditure. It is possible for only a part of this allowance to be claimed but it would depend on the particular circumstances as to whether or not one did so. (These are no longer generally applicable for expenditure incurred after 31 March 1986 but they are referred to here for the sake of completeness.)

(2) A *writing-down allowance* each year available during the life of the asset or until all expenditure has been allowed.

(3) A *balancing charge or allowance* on the disposal of the asset or at the end of the trade. The principle here is

that the total allowances given over the lifetime of the asset should not exceed the amount of actual expenditure incurred after allowing for any sale proceeds. If the amount given by way of allowances is less than the amount spent, the difference is a *balancing allowance*. If the allowances exceed the amount spent, the difference is brought into the income tax assessment by way of a *balancing charge*. If the asset is sold at a profit, the amount brought back into charge will not exceed the original allowances given but the excess may be charged to capital gains tax.

The allowance is normally set against taxable profits but if a loss has been incurred the capital allowances can be used to augment that loss or turn a profit into a loss. If the allowances exceed the profit thereby creating a loss, this loss can be relieved as described above at 2.6. Claims for capital allowances should be considered carefully because there is little point in claiming maximum allowances if this means that personal allowances will not be fully utilized. Any balance of expenditure remaining after a partial first-year allowance has been claimed is allocated to a capital expenditure 'pool' and relief is available by way of writing-down allowances as described above. Therefore, the expense of providing the asset for the purpose of using that asset within the business is, sooner or later, fully allowed against the profits which the asset assists in creating. However, if an allowance has been rashly claimed so that it displaces personal allowances, which are therefore lost for ever, the net after-tax cost of providing that capital asset is higher than it need have been.

3.2 PLANT AND MACHINERY

This is certainly the most common of the capital allowances claimed. The words 'plant and machinery' are not defined in the Taxes Acts but the meaning has been considered on a number of occasions by the courts. In a very old workman's compensation case it was stated:

> 'There is no definition of plant in the Act; but, in its ordinary sense, it includes whatever apparatus is used by a businessman for carrying on his business – not his stock-in-trade which he buys or makes for sale; but all goods and chattels, fixed or movable, live or dead, which he keeps for permanent employment in his business.'

More recently attention has been given to the question as to whether the asset concerned performs a *function* in the carrying on of the trade (so as to qualify for capital allowances) or whether it forms part of the *setting* in which the trade is carried on (so as not to so qualify). In deciding the matter the courts have given increasing emphasis to the application of this 'functional' test.

For instance, the courts declined to interfere with the Appeal Commissioners' decision that lighting and décor, etc. in hotels were plant because they contributed to 'creating' the right atmosphere in the bars and restaurant areas although part of the trade was the provision of accommodation. Again, the courts have accepted that certain electrical installations in a building are not plant on the grounds that the building would not be fit for use without, for example, a basic lighting system which could therefore be treated as part of the setting. However, in 'plant' they still included extra lighting systems for display units and high intensity lighting which might be required in an office area. Whether an item is plant or not is a question of fact which may have to be decided by the Commissioners hearing an appeal against the Revenue approach. The courts will not overrule a decision reached by the Commissioners except on a point of law, for example if the Commissioners have applied the wrong test or have come to a conclusion which they could not reasonably have come to on the evidence before them.

The Revenue view when considering whether expenditure has been incurred on capital items may be summarized as follows:

(1) It is necessary to look at the disputed object in order to see what it is and then consider what, in the context of the business carried on, its *function* is.

(2) Décor is plant where the Commissioners find that it helps to create atmosphere or ambience which it is an important function of the company's particular trade to provide for its customers to enjoy.

(3) Something which becomes part of the premises

instead of merely embellishing them is not plant except in rare cases where the premises themselves are plant.

(4)   The character of a disputed object is essentially a question of fact and degree for determination by the Commissioners.

Set out in Appendix G is a list of some of the items which have been recognized as plant and machinery for tax purposes and which should assist in determining whether allowances may be due. It should be emphasized, however, that this is only for general guidance and each case will need to be considered on its own merits.

The principle of disallowing entertainment expenditure for UK customers extends to disallowing capital allowances on any assets used for such entertainment. The asset is treated as being in use otherwise than for the purposes of the trade.

3.3   FIRST-YEAR AND WRITING-DOWN ALLOWANCES

As already mentioned in 3.1, first-year allowances have largely been phased out as regards expenditure incurred after 31 March 1986. However, these are referred to here as they may still be of importance in relation to expenditure incurred earlier. As a general principle first-year and writing-down allowances are generally given for the accounting period in which the expenditure was incurred. Usually the date of the invoice is used to determine which period the acquisition should fall into.

It is however vital to be able to establish that there is a *genuine* acquisition of the plant concerned, with a transfer of title and preferably an actual transfer of possession, at the time stated on the invoice, so as to be able to substantiate a claim for allowances by reference to that date. This can be particularly important where plant is being acquired shortly before the end of an accounting period.

Up to 13 March 1984 it was possible to claim a first-year allowance of up to 100% for expenditure on plant and machinery. However these allowances have now been phased out: between 14 March 1984 and 31 March 1985 they were available at 75%, and up to 31 March 1986 at 50%. After that date only a writing-down allowance of 25% on the declining balance will be given. Here again the importance of determining the date when the expenditure is incurred is self-evident.

Normally expenditure on plant goes into a single *pool* for these purposes; sale proceeds of plant sold or scrapped are credited to this pool so reducing the amount on which allowances may be given. Where the sale proceeds exceed the balance of expenditure brought forward, the difference is charged to tax as a *balancing charge*. The effect of these rules is illustrated in the following example relating to a business that has been established for a number of years.

EXAMPLE 6

	Pool of expenditure £	Allowances/ (balancing charge) £
Balance of expenditure b/fwd at 1 May 1985	500	
Writing-down allowance at 25%	125	125
	375	
Expenditure in year to 30 April 1986 Period 1 May 1985 to 31 March 1986	2,000	
Forward	2,000 375	125
First-year allowance at 50%	1,000 1,000	1,000
		(1987/88) £1,125
	1,375	
Sale proceeds in year to 30 April 1987	775	
	600	

Writing-down allowance at 25%	150	(1988/89)	£150
	450		
Sale proceeds in year to 30 April 1988	650		
Balancing charge	£200	(1989/90)	£(200)

For expenditure incurred after 31 March 1986 on plant having an anticipated life of less than five years (typically 'hi-tech' items), it is provided that these may be dealt with outside the normal pool, so permitting a quicker utilization of allowances.

As shown above, the basis periods for capital allowances arising in income tax cases are normally the same as those for profits, but there are occasions when this is not so, particularly at the commencement or cessation of a business. On the commencement of a business or where the accounting period was the basis period for more than one year of assessment the rule was that first-year allowances were given only once and in the earliest possible income tax year.

If plant is used for business and partly for private purposes, the allowances available are reduced in such proportion as is reasonable in relation to the private element.

If plant is purchased for some use other than trade use

and later brought into trade use, perhaps when the trade
is being commenced, the trader will be entitled to a
writing-down allowance from that point based on its
market value at that time.

The term 'plant and machinery' also includes *motor
vehicles* but only certain types qualified for the first-year
allowance. These were goods vehicles, e.g. lorries, vehicles
unsuitable to be used as private vehicles (or not commonly
used as such) and vehicles provided wholly or mainly for
hire to the general public.

There is no first-year allowance on other motor cars but
if the car is bought by the business and it is used during
the course of carrying on the business the 25% writing-
down allowance will be granted. The car is put into a
separate pool if the initial cost is more than £8,000. If this
is the case the writing-down allowance is restricted to a
maximum £2,000 each year until the amount brought
forward falls below £8,000 when the 25% rate of allowance
becomes operative. Where all the car expenses have been
claimed in the accounts and there is an element of private
motoring expenses, an adjustment will need to be made
in the tax computation and to the writing-down allowances
to arrive at the taxable profit, as there is no entitlement to
tax allowances for the private use of a car.

A lessor of motor cars is also entitled to 25% writing-
down allowances on a reducing balance basis with a
maximum allowance of £2,000 per car per annum as
explained above. Lease rentals paid by the lessee are fully
deductible in arriving at taxable profit except where the
price of the car exceeds £8,000. Where this is the case there
is a permanent disallowance of a proportion of the leasing

charge. The sum allowed as a deduction is reduced in the
proportion which £8,000 together with one-half of the
excess bears to the original retail price of the car.

EXAMPLE 7

A car, the cost of which when new would have been
£12,000, is leased by an employer for £3,000 p.a. The
amount of the lease rental allowed is calculated as
follows:

$$\frac{£8,000 + (£12,000 - £8,000)/2}{£12,000} \times £3,000 = \underline{\underline{£2,500}}$$

Rental permanently disallowed   £500

Therefore, where a car costs £12,000 new, 1/6th of the
rental payments are permanently disallowed.

This permanent disallowance does make leasing of more
expensive cars disadvantageous.

Where a car is bought under a hire purchase arrangement
capital allowances are available on it on the same terms as
a car brought for cash. The date of purchase is the date
the contract is signed. The element of interest inherent in
hire purchase instalments is an allowable trading deduction for tax purposes and as a matter of Inland Revenue
practice is not subject to the restriction described above
for cars costing more than £8,000.

3.4 INDUSTRIAL BUILDINGS

Industrial buildings and structures which qualify for *industrial buildings allowances* ('IBAs') are broadly those buildings or structures in use for the purposes of a trade of manufacturing, storage, mining or power production. A warehouse used to store raw materials which are to be subject to some manufacturing process is included in this definition, as is a warehouse that is used by a manufacturer to store finished products pending distribution. Where a warehouse is used partly to store manufactured goods and partly to store purchased goods, the tax treatment will depend upon the facts of the case. Provided no identifiable area of the warehouse could be regarded as used solely for the storage of goods of either category a claim should succeed in full. Where a warehouse contains one section for manufactured goods and one section for purchased goods then it is likely only a proportional claim will succeed.

A building which is close to a seaport or airport and used to store goods imported into the UK through that port may also qualify for the allowance.

Specifically excluded are offices, showrooms, hotels, retail shops and similar premises. A warehouse owned by a wholesaler who does not carry on any manufacturing process is not an industrial building. Where part of a building qualifies as industrial but the rest does not, the allowances are given proportionately except where the cost of the non-qualifying part is 25% or less of the total cost in which case the non-qualifying element is ignored.

The allowances are available to individuals incurring the capital expenditure not only if they occupy the building for the purposes of their own trade but also if they lease the building and the lessee or ultimate lessee uses it for a qualifying purpose as defined above.

The expenditure that would qualify includes ground levelling, construction of the building, quantity surveyors' and architects' fees, a basic internal electrical wiring system, ventilation and switchgear equipment if plant and machinery allowances could not be obtained, security fencing and road construction. The cost of the land itself is excluded.

As with capital allowances on plant and machinery, initial allowances have been phased out. For expenditure incurred up to 31 March 1986, an *initial allowance* of 25% could have been claimed.

A *writing-down allowance* of 4% of cost on a *straight line* basis is available until the balance of expenditure has been fully relieved. This allowance is given first in the year in which the building is brought into use and continues to be given annually until the whole cost has been allowed or the building is sold.

When an industrial building that has been in use for less than 25 years (50 in the case of expenditure incurred before 6 November 1962) is sold or otherwise disposed of the proceeds are compared with the unallowed residue of expenditure brought forward. Any excess of sale proceeds (up to original cost) over the residue is taxed by way of a balancing charge as profit, whereas any excess of sale proceeds over original cost will be taxed as a capital gain. Conversely, a balancing allowance is given as a deduction from taxable profits where the proceeds are less than the residue.

Where the building is more than 25 (or 50 if built before November 1962) years old a sale does not give rise to a balancing adjustment at all.

Purchasers of an *unused* building are entitled to initial and writing-down allowances. If they buy it from someone carrying on a trade of constructing buildings for sale, the IBA is given on the purchase price, whereas if they buy it from someone else (e.g. a property dealer) the IBA is given on the lower of the purchase price and the constructor's sale price. Expenditure incurred on purchasing a *second-hand* industrial building, i.e. one that has been used by a previous owner, does not qualify for an initial allowance. If the building is less than 25 (or 50 if built before November 1962) years old then broadly speaking the lower of the purchase cost and the original cost is given by way of writing-down allowances at an even rate over the balance of the unexpired term of 25 (or 50) years. No allowance is due if the building is more than 25 (or 50) years old.

In certain circumstances the freeholder and a leaseholder holding a lease of more than fifty years can decide between them who should be entitled to the IBAs. Where a freeholder has incurred the expenditure and he grants a lease for a capital sum it is possible to elect that the leaseholder has the entitlement to the IBAs. This will be on the lesser of the expenditure incurred by the freeholder and the capital sum paid by the leaseholder. The same applies where a leaseholder grants a long underlease. This election is particularly appropriate where the lessor is a non-taxpaying institution or has an abundance of tax losses.

As mentioned in 2.8.1, expenditure on many types of commercial buildings (not just industrial buildings) in *enterprise zones* ranks for a 100% initial allowance (or, if not claimed in full, for a 25% writing-down allowance of cost on a straight-line basis).

3.5   AGRICULTURAL BUILDINGS

Capital allowances can be claimed for expenditure on the construction of new agricultural buildings and on agricultural works such as fencing, draining and land reclamation. Initial and writing-down allowances are given primarily against assessments on agricultural or forestry income, but where allowances exceed the income of the year of assessment they may be carried forward without time limit against future such income. Alternatively, and subject to a claim being made within two years of the end of the year of assessment, they may be set against other income of that year or the following year. For expenditure incurred up to 31 March 1986, an initial allowance of up to 20% and a writing-down allowance of 10% on a straight-line basis could have been claimed, but these have now been withdrawn. For expenditure incurred after 31 March 1986, only a writing-down allowance of 4% of cost on a straight-line basis is available.

Where property is transferred or there is a change of tenant the transferee normally takes over the writing-down allowances for the remainder of the writing-down period. The allowance for the year of sale is apportioned. No balancing charge is levied nor are balancing allowances given in this case. However, where the expenditure was incurred after 31 March 1986, on a subsequent disposal, transferor and transferee may jointly elect to have the property treated as disposed of at its market value so as to give rise to a balancing adjustment; this can also be done where a building, etc. is demolished. This facility can be helpful for assets having a relatively short life.

Where the expenditure is on houses, not more than one-third of a farmhouse or the proprietor's house qualifies for relief but this can be reduced if only a smaller proportion of the house is used for the purposes of farming. The whole cost of cottages occupied by farmworkers normally qualifies.

3.6 GRANTS

Where grants or subsidies are made available by a development agency they will usually have to be deducted in arriving at total expenditure eligible for capital allowances.

There are certain grants, however, such as regional development grants and their Northern Ireland equivalent which are not deducted, and capital allowances can be claimed on the full qualifying expenditure (see 2.8 above regarding government assistance).

3.7 VALUE ADDED TAX

With the exception of motor cars where the input tax is generally not deductible (see 2.7.1), VAT paid on purchases of capital items by a trader who is registered for VAT purposes is available for credit as input tax in the usual way. On the disposal of capital assets VAT is chargeable on sale proceeds as output tax. Capital allowances are available on the net cost to the business only, and the net proceeds of disposal only are taken into account in caculating balancing charges or allowances.

However, it is proposed in the case of partly exempt businesses (see 2.7.4) to modify these rules at some future time. Instead of the restriction of input tax on capital assets being calculated by reference to the VAT position for that year only, it will be adjusted over a five-year period. It is far from clear how this new basis is intended to operate in practice.

4 When the Business is in Business

David Wiltshire is now running his business, and this is likely to give rise to a whole series of new challenges such as the need for forward planning, identifying business strategies, budgeting and management reporting, cash forecasting and control, etc. Inevitably tax considerations continue to be vitally important.

4.1 RAISING FINANCE FOR EXPANSION

When a business is doing well working capital required to finance stocks and production can become woefully insufficient: this can in turn restrict the pace at which development takes place, and business opportunities may be lost. Few fast growing businesses are able to finance their expansion wholly from existing resources, so new money is generally required.

Planning for the future is essential because, as a rule, it is fairly easy to obtain finance in advance of the need to spend it, but people are less keen to lend money where it is needed to pay out liabilities already incurred.

It is also important to ensure that short-term borrowing is not obtained to build business premises which will be used in the business for 20 years or more unless the projected cash flow indicates that repayment will be possible.

The primary source of further capital injections must be the proprietor himself. When the funds exist to cover the shortfall where profits cannot finance new development this is the easy answer and the proprietor retains control of his business. In the situation where this is not so, raising the capital necessary to expand the business can be difficult. An existing proprietor may not wish to admit partners purely because they are able to finance the business, and investors may not wish to have the responsibilities such a situation carries.

Another primary source of external finance is likely to be the bank. Generally, the bank will require a fixed charge over specified assets or a floating charge in respect of all assets comprised in the business. Remember that where substantial security is provided the flexibility for arranging new borrowings in the future may be limited. To ensure that a good working relationship is retained, bank managers should be provided with all the business information they require such as accounts and projections on a timely basis, and the agreed borrowing limits should not be breached. Where further financing is required forecasts of the expected achievements of the business should be given. Where these forecasts are over-optimistic and the achievements are short of those expected the future willingness of bank managers to make a loan where security for the bank is not total may be jeopardized. However, do not become too dependent upon any one source of finance – always be prepared to consider what other opportunities there are in the market place.

When fixed assets are being acquired it might be preferable, rather than to tie up working capital in assets such as cars or buildings, to enter into hire purchase or leasing agreements. Generally, all revenue expenditure in connection with these two forms is allowable in calculating taxable profit. Capital allowances will be available from the outset with hire purchase, because at the end of the agreement legal title to the asset passes to the hirer. With a lease, title does not pass at the end of the term, so that what is being acquired is the right to use the asset rather than the asset itself, the lessor retaining legal ownership of the asset throughout. The benefits of the capital allowances which become available to the lessor should be reflected in the leasing charge.

4.2   CHANGE OF ACCOUNTING DATE

Usually, once a business has commenced trade the accounting date that is decided on at the outset is retained during the business's life. However, there may sometimes be good reasons for changing the accounting date. It is possible that the type and scope of the business changes gradually with the trading conditions found in the market and that necessitates a different approach. For example, if the business is seasonal, it may be more convenient to move the accounting date to a time when stock and work in progress are low, so reducing the chore of stocktaking.

There may be a merger of two businesses to form a more substantial one, in which case one, or indeed neither, party's accounting date may be considered appropriate for the new business. Or there may be tax reasons such as obtaining a greater cash flow advantage by delaying further the time between the end of the accounting year and the date that any tax liability needs to be paid.

A change of accounting date involves some complex considerations which are outside the scope of a book of this size. In particular, it must be recognized that the Inland Revenue may take a close interest in the consequences of a change, especially if, as may be the case, it results in an actual reduction in tax liabilities. It is therefore essential that any change in accounting date can be justified on commercial grounds other than the saving of tax.

Whilst any decision to change the accounting date can be taken only after making detailed calculations with the benefit of up-to-date accounts and accurate trading forecasts, as a general indication a change may be advantageous in the following circumstances:

(1) Where the present accounting date is later in the tax year (e.g. 31 December or 31 March) and profits are expected to *rise*, moving the accounting date *forward* to a date early in the following tax year (e.g. 30 April).
(2) Where the present accounting date is early in the tax year (e.g. 30 April) and profits are expected to *fall*,

shortening the accounting period so as to end in the
same tax year as previously (e.g. 31 March).

4.3 ROLLOVER RELIEF

As the business develops assets used for business purposes
may from time to time have to be replaced or, due to the
expansion of the business, new premises will need to be
acquired. In such a situation it is quite likely that, due to
the effects of inflation, a chargeable gain may arise on the
excess of sale proceeds over original cost; this can apply
particularly to buildings. If such gains were taxed in full
this would bleed money away out of the business which
would then not be able to reinvest and its expansion might
be inhibited. However, provided certain conditions are
met, the tax code allows any resulting capital gains tax
liability to be deferred.

Traders disposing of qualifying assets used exclusively
for the purposes of their trade who spend all or part of
the proceeds on other assets used in the same way may
elect to defer some or all of the capital gains tax arising by
deducting the chargeable gain from the cost of the new
assets. To qualify, expenditure on the new asset must be
incurred one year before or three years after disposal of
the old assets (the Revenue have discretion to extend these
time limits in suitable circumstances).

Only the following classes of assets may qualify for
rollover relief:

(1) Land and buildings occupied (as well as used) only for the purposes of the trade.
(2) Fixed plant or machinery which does not form part of a building.
(3) Ships, aircraft and hovercraft.
(4) Goodwill.

Both the old and new assets must fall within the above classes but need not necessarily be of the same class.

In one situation a factory site had been bought by a trading company which proposed to build a factory. However, after obtaining planning permission, it decided to build elsewhere. It was held that no relief was due on any increase in value of that land as it had not been used *and* occupied for the purposes of the trade.

The interpretation placed on 'fixed plant or machinery' at (2) above has been clarified by the courts to mean 'fixed plant or *fixed* machinery'. Therefore, earthmoving equipment, combine harvesters or tractors, or similar *mobile* machinery will not qualify for this relief.

EXAMPLE 8

David acquired land and buildings for £45,000 in July 1985. On 15 May 1988 this property was sold realizing £90,000 after incidental costs of disposal. Further property was purchased for £120,000 on 29 May 1988. The Revenue accepted that rollover relief was available for the gain arising on the sale of the old property. The new property realized £165,000 when it was sold and not replaced on 18 July 1990. Ignoring indexation:

(a)   The chargeable gain on the disposal of the first
      asset would be:

	£
Disposal proceeds	90,000
Less: Cost	45,000
Gross gain	45,000
Less: Rollover relief	45,000
Chargeable gain	£ *nil*

(b)   The cost for tax purposes of the second asset is:

Acquisition cost	120,000
Less: Rollover relief	45,000
	£75,000

Note that this deduction does *not* affect the amount on
which capital allowances (if applicable) may be claimed.

(c)   The chargeable gain on the disposal of the second
      asset is:

Disposal proceeds	165,000
Less: Reduced cost of new asset	75,000
Chargeable gain	£90,000

In the situation where only part of the net sale proceeds

are reinvested, a measure of cash is available to meet a
capital gains tax liability. Only the part of the gain that is
reinvested will attract rollover relief. If in the example
above David had reinvested only £60,000 on the disposal
of the first asset, the position would have been as follows:

Gain on first asset (as above)	£45,000

Part consideration not applied in acquiring new asset:

	£
Disposal proceeds	90,000
Part reinvested	60,000
Chargeable gain	£30,000

Therefore £15,000 attracts rollover relief and £30,000
attracts a capital gains tax charge.

Where the gain arises on the disposal of old assets
acquired before 6 April 1965 only part of that gain is
chargeable. Generally, the gain arising on an asset is
apportioned evenly over the time the asset is owned and
that relating to ownership prior to the inception of capital
gains tax on 6 April 1965 is exempt.

Where the new asset acquired is a *wasting* asset (i.e. it
has an expected life of less than fifty years), or will become
so within ten years, the gain on the disposal of the old
asset may be rolled over only temporarily and will become
chargeable to tax on the earliest of the following events:

(a)   the disposal of the new asset; *or*
(b)   the date the new asset ceases to be used in a trade carried on by the trader; *or*
(c)   ten years after its acquisition.

However, if before any of the above events a further asset is acquired which is *not* a wasting asset, the trader may substitute the new asset for the wasting asset in his rollover claim so that normal rollover relief rules will apply.

Where land is acquired from a trader under a compulsory purchase order and leased back to the vendor the three-year time limit in which a claim has to be made after the sale of an asset is extended by the Revenue to one year after the land ceases to be used for the trade, provided it is always intended that the sale proceeds will be used to acquire qualifying assets.

A gain realized on the disposal of an asset used in a trade can be rolled over into an asset acquired for a successive trade. The official view as to what is a 'successive' trade in broad terms is that where a trader ceases carrying on one trade and commences carrying on another trade he will be regarded as carrying them on successively where the interval between the trades does not exceed three years.

4.4 TAKING ON EMPLOYEES

4.4.1 Staff requirements

As the level of business activities increases, more people, and people with particular skills, will be needed to cope with the volume of business. People employed while the business is in its relative infancy will play a major role in the way the business develops and their response to change and growth will be very important. However, there is likely to come a time when it is necessary to recruit new staff. At this time thought may have to be given to developing specialist functions carried on within the business. Also, people interested in joining will need to have some idea of what is expected of them and how they can assist in the continuing development not only of the business, but also of themselves, and how they will be rewarded for their efforts. The more important features to be looked at in a potential recruit will be age, education, qualifications, experience, intelligence, motivation, personality and appearance.

Once you have decided upon the type of person you require, do you interview prospective candidates yourself or do you leave this to an organization specializing in such work? Agencies can be expensive but when the time spent interviewing and the possible effects of less time spent ensuring the proper running of the business are taken into account it may be found to be money well spent.

It has been said before that people, generally, will look to see what contribution they can make to the success of the business and they would expect to be rewarded accordingly. Consequently the establishment of a recognized pay and career structure is very important. Some business people argue that staff should be paid enough to keep them but no more. This is shortsighted because in time staff will realize this and if they feel they are not being suitably rewarded for the efforts they are putting into the business their commitment and achievement will be less.

4.4.2 Employment law

New staff being taken on have a certain level of employment protection under the law. For instance, particular periods of notice have to be given before employment can be terminated and care should be taken to ensure that non-compliance with the law when dealing with staff does not result in wasted time and effort which could be better spent in developing the business; and, of course, professional fees may be incurred in defending your case. Broadly, the rules are that if new recruits turn out to be unsatisfactory their employment can be terminated without any minimum period of notice up to four weeks after the employment commences. After that initial period the following periods of notice are required:

(1) For periods of continuous employment of less than two years, not less than one week's notice.
(2) For periods of continuous employment of more than two years but less than twelve years, not less than one

week's notice for each of those years of continuous employment.

(3) For a period of continuous employment of twelve years or more, not less than twelve weeks' notice.

There are times when an employee can be dismissed without notice, such as in a case of gross misconduct, but professional advice should always be taken in such cases.

To ensure that both yourself and your staff are fully aware of the conditions under which they are employed, a written contract detailing the conditions of employment should be signed by both parties and a copy retained by each. The contract should include details of the parties involved, the date of commencement of the employment, computation of pay and frequency of payment – i.e. weekly or monthly – definition of hours to be worked, holiday entitlement, rules relating to sickness and sick pay, details of any pension schemes, the notice period required, the employee's job title, disciplinary rules and, if agreed beforehand, the date that the contract is to expire.

4.4.3 Salary package

The question then arises as to whether there should be some incentives built into the pay structure to encourage extra effort. As far as employers are concerned, what is important to them is the net cost to their business of employing a particular individual, and it is in their own interests to get the best out of that individual. Because of the way the UK tax and national insurance systems work it can sometimes be beneficial for the employee, without incurring any extra real expense for the employer, to have a flexible salary package that might include bonus payments (see 4.4.4), profit related pay (4.4.5), cars (4.4.6), pension schemes (4.4.7) and non-cash benefits.

4.4.4 Bonus schemes

The principle here is that employees' earnings can be related to output and their contribution to the success of the business. It is possibly better to relate such schemes to a small group's performance as this will encourage cross-pollination of ideas and cooperation amongst the workforce.

4.4.5 Profit related pay

In his Budget speech on 18 March 1986, the Chancellor of the Exchequer announced a new initiative whereby employees who joined in a scheme with their employer to take a part of their pay in the form of a share of profits could obtain certain tax incentives. Following consultations with representative bodies the necessary legislation was included in the second 1987 Finance Act.

The intention is that one half of profit related pay (PRP) will be free of income tax up to the point where PRP forms 20% of an employee's pay or £3,000 per annum, whichever is lower. It is anticipated that a married man on average earnings would receive relief amounting to approximately £6 per week. The employer must register a scheme with the Revenue before it comes into operation. The scheme must relate to an identifiable 'employment unit' which can be the whole business or a sub-unit of it.

Employers will generally be free to design their own schemes but certain basic qualifications will be required:
(1) There must be a clear relationship between the PRP pool of the employment unit and its audited profits. This may be achieved in either of two ways:
    (a) the total PRP pool can be a simple *proportion of profits*; or
    (b) the pool can be defined as a sum of money which varies in line with *year on year changes in profits*.
'Profits for this purpose would normally be the audited after-tax profits of the employment unit as defined in the Companies Act 1985. These may be adjusted where this is considered appropriate but such adjustments must be applied consistently.
(2) New recruits and part-timers may be excluded. Otherwise, at least 80% of the employees, *other than controlling directors*, within the employment unit must be covered by the scheme.
(3) When the scheme commences, it must be seen to anticipate that where profits remain the same, the total PRP produced by the formula under (1) will be at least 5% of the participating employees' total pay.
(4) The scheme must run for at least one year.

Obviously, any decision to implement a PRP scheme has to be made by the employer, probably after consultation with his employees. It is suggested that a scheme could be introduced into pay bargains instead of a conventional increase in pay, possibly involving the conversion of some existing pay into PRP. It may also be possible to include current profit sharing schemes, provided that the qualifications set out above can be met.

The Inland Revenue have set up a separate office to deal with PRP, whose address is

Profit Related Pay Office,
Inland Revenue,
St Mungo's Road,
Cumbernauld,
Glasgow G67 1YZ.

Any employer who wishes to apply for registration of a PRP scheme may obtain an application form from that address. The Revenue hope to issue guidance notes on PRP during September.

4.4.6 Cars

Despite the imposition of a tax charge on the employee relating to the provision of a car, this is still a very tax efficient way of rewarding keen employees. In view of the fact that this, like other non-cash benefits, is not chargeable to Class 1 national insurance contributions, it can be expected to become an increasingly attractive part of an employee's salary package, having regard to the changes in the structure of employers' contributions brought in in October 1985.

The significant benefit for employees is that they do not need to find the capital necessary to purchase the car and they save on the usual standing charges. Where fuel is supplied, a further tax charge for this benefit may be levied on the employee, but provided the net cost of this charge is less than the value of fuel received the employee continues to benefit. The tax consequences of being provided with a company car as far as the employee is concerned is covered in detail in *The Touche Ross Tax Guide to Pay and Perks*.

The arrangements for charging VAT on petrol supplied to employees for private motoring, to take effect from 6 April 1987, have already been described in 2.7.2.

4.4.7 Pension schemes

The provision of a good pension scheme can attract good calibre staff but can also be a heavy drain on the business's resources. Where a scheme is set up a decision has to be made as to whether the scheme should be contracted out of the State scheme. This means in effect that the employer provides the benefits that the State would otherwise have provided and in return both the employee and the employer pay Class 1 national insurance contributions at a lower rate – see Appendix C. Increases in the level of contributions payable in recent years have generally meant that this option has proved less attractive.

The cost of administering a group scheme by a small firm need not be too high depending upon the number of staff involved. Under a small self-administered scheme the administration and the management of the investments of the pension fund are undertaken by trustees who can be nominated by the proprietor.

A small scheme is one with less than twelve members. This number can in practice be higher as the Revenue will ignore relatively low paid employees where their inclusion would just breach the twelve-member limit. These schemes are beneficial where the annual contribution is approximately £10,000 and where, at inception, employees are unlikely to retire in the near future. They allow a good deal of investment freedom; direct control of the investments of the pension scheme is with the trustees, of which the proprietor will normally be one; and they have full powers to place pension money in a very wide range of investments. It is also usually possible to change investment managers at relatively low cost, and there is generally less risk to the business's cash flow position as there is a measure of flexibility on the timing of contributions.

However, there are certain disadvantages. Not insignificant costs may be incurred on the level of administration necessary. Also, the investment abilities of the proprietor and his co-trustees will ultimately be reflected in the level of contributions necessarily paid into the scheme to ensure that the minimum level of benefits promised to employees under the scheme is met.

Before giving approval to such a scheme the Superannuation Funds Office of the Inland Revenue will require that one of the trustees of the fund is a *pensioneer trustee*; this has to be an individual or a body, independent of the firm, well experienced in the field of occupational pension schemes. On appointment the pensioneer trustee is required to give certain undertakings as to the winding up of the scheme and as to its management generally.

Insurance companies also operate insured schemes in return for a minimum level of contribution. The administration of the scheme is then undertaken by the insurance company. The main types of insured schemes are:

(1) With profits – the pension fund is increased each year by the addition of bonuses which cannot be taken away once declared.
(2) Non-profit – useful when the amount of pension at pension age needs to be guaranteed and more appropriate where there is a short time to go before retirement.
(3) Unit linked – the value of the scheme fluctuates with the value of the underlying assets; capable of good growth but more risky.
(4) Deposit administration – operated in much the same way as a bank deposit account and so steady growth is the main characteristic.

When considering entering the pensions market specialist professional advice, in the legal and taxation field as well as in the pension area itself, should be obtained before proceeding.

Certainly, the attraction of having a pension scheme will vary depending upon the circumstances of individual employees. Young employees who do not expect to stay with a particular employer for life consider their value limited, whereas older employees who can be expected to remain are likely to value them more highly.

Schemes may be contributory or non-contributory. The latter cost the employer more or provide lower benefits. Individual employees can contribute up to a maximum of 15% of their remuneration into a pension scheme in addition to the employer's contributions. In many cases members of approved occupational pension schemes are required under the scheme rules to contribute less than

15%; it may be possible for individual employees to make up all or part of the difference by paying *additional voluntary contributions* either connected with the main pension scheme or into a separate plan.

An occupational pension scheme may also provide for *personal injury* cover for employees, either by way of lump sum payments for loss of life or limbs, or (perhaps less desirably because of the long-term commitment that may be incurred) by disability pension payments.

The government is concerned to promote the setting up of occupational pension schemes; as an alternative, with effect from the beginning of 1988, employees may organise their own pension arrangements with or without the involvement of their employers. More information on this topic is contained in Chapter 10 of *The Touche Ross Tax Guide to Pay and Perks 1987/88* by Bill Packer and Elaine Baker (Papermac, 1987).

4.4.8 Keyman insurance

It may be desirable to provide the business with some protection against the loss through untimely death of the services of certain key employees, where this could disrupt the firm's operations for a time.

This can usually be arranged through a suitable form of term assurance policy. On the basis that any sum paid out under the policy is brought into the business accounts as a trading receipt, the premium payments will be deductible for tax purposes. Where the policy proceeds are not taxed in this way, the premium payments will not be deductible. It should be emphasized that not claiming the premiums as a business expense does *not*, of itself, prevent the policy proceeds from being taxed in due course.

It is not possible for the proprietor of a business such as David Wiltshire to set up such a keyman insurance arrangement for himself and obtain the benefit of tax relief.

4.4.9   The proprietor's wife

One person who would have been involved in the business since it commenced is David's wife Elaine. When the business was getting started, Elaine was employed mainly to assist by undertaking secretarial duties and the opportunity was taken, by paying her a salary that could be seen to be commercially reasonable, of retaining funds within the family and reducing the potential tax charge on business profits. She will have seen the business develop and her responsibilities will have increased accordingly. She has developed a thorough understanding of the business and probably knows most of the suppliers and customers.

At the outset when the amount of time she spent in the business was relatively low, it would have been appropriate to pay her a salary below the lower of the wife's earned income allowance and the lower earnings limit for national insurance purposes. For 1987/88 these limits are £46·63 and £39 a week respectively; thus a weekly wage of £38 would attract no charge to tax or national insurance in Elaine's hands and (provided that it could be justified on commercial grounds in relation to the hours worked and the duties performed by her) would be fully allowable for tax purposes in David's accounts.

As the business develops and Elaine's involvement in it increases, it may be appropriate to consider paying her a substantially higher salary. The first prerequisite is that the amount paid must still be commercially justifiable and no greater than David would have to pay an unrelated employee to do the same job; if this test is satisfied then the full amount of Elaine's salary, plus the employer's national insurance contributions that would now have to be paid and any pension scheme contributions, would be deductible.

Some overall tax saving, depending on the level of David's and Elaine's earnings, may be achieved by using the *wife's earnings election*. This has the effect of taxing their earnings as if they were separate single persons, instead of aggregating them as is normally required. Although David thereby loses the higher personal allowance for a married man, Elaine is entitled to the full basic rate band (up to £17,900 for 1987/88) with the higher rates being applied separately to their incomes. Although the decision as to whether this election is of advantage or not depends on the individuals' exact circumstances, it should be considered where their joint earnings exceed a certain level (£26,870 in 1987/88). The election must be made jointly by both spouses, not earlier than six months before and not later than twelve months after the end of the tax year for which it is to apply. Thereafter it continues in operation until revoked; again this must be done by both parties jointly, not later than twelve months after the end of the tax year for which it is to be withdrawn.

If Elaine is paid at a rate at or above the limit set for national insurance contribution purposes (at present £39 per week), compulsory contributions will be due from her and from David as her employer (see Appendix C). While these will entitle her to certain benefits under the social security system, in particular to a retirement pension in her own right, they may be considered to be of limited value in practice.

This arrangement is dealt with in more detail in *The Touche Ross Tax Guide to Pay and Perks 1987/88* by Bill Packer and Elaine Baker (Papermac, 1987).

4.4.10 PAYE

Where staff are employed there is a responsibility on all employers to operate PAYE. This is the scheme for the collection of tax on employee earnings. Its aim is to deduct tax from each payment of emoluments, the deduction rising and falling as the pay rises and falls, so that at the end of the income tax year the tax deducted during the year is correct having regard to the employee's personal circumstances, and no further action is normally necessary.

The backbone of the system is the 'cumulative' principle (described in 2.2) under which, as the tax year progresses, running (cumulative) totals are kept of the amount of emoluments received from the beginning of the tax year and of the tax deducted. Each time employers pay salaries and wages they deduct (or refund) an amount of tax which will keep the cumulative figure deducted for each employee correct. They are supplied with tax tables by the Inland Revenue to enable them to do this on a weekly or monthly basis, whichever is appropriate. The total of the tax deducted, less any tax refunded for each month, must be paid to the Collector of Taxes within fourteen days of the end of each tax month. The amount paid over also includes any national insurance contributions which may be due (see 4.4.11).

To enable employers to deduct the correct amount of tax each week or each month, they are supplied by the Revenue with a *coding* for each employee. This is based on the employee's personal allowances and other reliefs but does not disclose to employers any personal information about him.

Details of pay, tax and national insurance contributions are entered on deduction working sheets which are completed by employers on each pay day. After 5 April each year employers send year end returns to the Collector of Taxes listing the employees and showing the total amount of tax deducted from each. They also provide each employee with a statement of his pay and tax for the year on form P60.

As well as processing the tax details for each employee, the Revenue pass on the details relating to their national insurance contributions to the Department of Health and Social Security for their records.

The Revenue issue a detailed booklet entitled *The Employer's Guide to PAYE* to each employer which contains a mass of information on the operation of the PAYE system. There is also more information on it in *The Touche Ross Tax Guide to Pay and Perks 1987/88* by Bill Packer and Elaine Baker (Papermac 1987).

The Inland Revenue have always had the power to inspect employers' records to satisfy themselves that PAYE is being properly applied against salaries and wages. In

recent years, with the increase in the provision of benefits
of all kinds to employees, the Revenue have considerably
increased the scope of their examinations in this area.
There are now approximately 700 specialist staff engaged
on this work in the field and the intention is that all
employers' records will be examined every three to five
years. These audit teams mainly concentrate on the payment of allowances, expenses and other cash items which
may give rise to a liability to account for PAYE tax and
also in appropriate circumstances to national insurance
contributions.

The Revenue are also giving increased attention to the
tax treatment of non-cash benefits; the examination of
these is normally dealt with by local Inspectors of Taxes.

Every employer is required to notify to the Inland
Revenue details of all benefits, expense payments and
allowances provided to or for each *higher paid employee* in
each tax year. A 'higher paid employee' is an employee
earning at a rate of £8,500 or more per annum including
the value of benefits and expenses reimbursed but after
deducting superannuation contributions. This is done by
completing a form P11D in respect of each person. To save
time and administration costs the employer may be granted
a *dispensation* from having to include routine expense
payments and benefits on forms P11D. For this purpose
the employer must satisfy the Inspector that all expenses
and payments received will be covered by an equivalent
amount of expense deductions. This requirement is strictly
applied and therefore only routine travelling, subsistence
and hotel expenses are normally covered. Where a dispensation is given the relevant expenses need not be included

in forms P11D nor in the income tax returns of employees. They are also ignored for the purposes of deciding whether or not an employee is over the £8,500 limit. However, a dispensation will not normally be granted where it has the effect of removing an employee from the 'higher paid' bracket to the category of an employee earning less than at the rate of £8,500 per annum so as to render certain benefits, e.g. use of a company car, no longer subject to tax. Where the employer is a *company*, these rules apply also to its *directors* regardless of the level of pay.

4.4.11   National insurance contributions

Although not strictly a tax, national insurance contributions are none the less a major cost to virtually all employers and employees.

Contributions under Class 1 are payable by all employees whose earnings exceed a certain amount per week or per month. The current rates (1987/88) are shown in Appendix C. Deductions are made through the PAYE system by the employer who also has to make a contribution, using tables issued by the Department of Health and Social Security. The contributions vary depending upon whether the employer is contracted in or out of the state scheme. If it is the latter the contributions are lower as there is no payment made to secure the earnings-related element of the state pension scheme.

The DHSS issue a number of very useful booklets that give excellent guidance on the whole range of national insurance contributions.

4.4.12 Statutory sick pay

With effect from 6 April 1983 employers have been respon-
sible for the payment of *statutory sick pay* ('SSP') to
employees where their sickness absence does not exceed
eight weeks in any tax year.

Where an employee, who is under pensionable age and
whose average weekly earnings are not less than the lower
earnings limit for national insurance purposes (currently
£39·00 per week), notifies his employer that he is sick, the
employer must in most circumstances make a payment to
him of SSP. This applies if the day in question:

(a) forms part of a period of four or more consecutive
days (including Sundays) of such sickness; note that
two periods are treated as one if the time between
them is not more than fourteen days; *and*

(b) falls within a period of entitlement subject to the
employee exhausting his or her maximum entitlement
of SSP of eight times the appropriate weekly amount
described below; *and*

(c) is a qualifying day, i.e. the day, or one of the days of
the week, which the employer and the employee
agree be classed as a qualifying day; these will
generally be the days on which the employee is
required to work, and for the majority of people will
be Monday to Friday; there must be at least one
qualifying day in each week.

There are different rates of SSP based on the employee's
normal weekly earnings. For the tax year 1987/88 the
weekly rates are as follows:

Normal weekly earnings	*Statutory sick pay*
Less than £39	Nil
£39–£76·49	£32·85
£76·50 or more	£47·20

Where an employer continues to pay an employee under the terms of his or her employment contract this payment in itself will be sufficient discharge of the employer's liability under the scheme, provided that it at least equals the weekly rates of SSP detailed above.

Employers can reclaim all SSP payments that they make to sick employees by deducting the gross amount paid to an employee from the monthly national insurance contributions that they would pay over to the Collector of Taxes when operating the PAYE scheme in the normal way. SSP is itself liable to PAYE and national insurance contributions.

Employers are required to keep records of payments of SSP and details of the sickness absence of all employees for examination by DHSS inspectors. The information employers need to keep, for a minimum of three years after the tax year to which they relate and for each employee separately, is:

(1) Dates of each period of sickness absence reported by employees.
(2) Dates when SSP was not paid, with reasons, including excluded employees, i.e. those earning at a rate less than the lower earnings limit.

(3) Details of the agreed working week, i.e. the days qualifying under the scheme;
(4) Details of SSP payments made.

A SSP scheme is another administrative burden imposed on employers, but one benefit of having to retain this detail is that employers may be able to control sickness absence more effectively than has perhaps been possible in the past.

The DHSS have produced a helpful booklet (NI 227) describing the workings of the scheme.

4.4.13 Statutory maternity pay

With effect from 6 April 1987 employers are also required to pay *statutory maternity pay* ('SMP') to pregnant women employees prior to their confinement where this is expected to fall on or after 21 June 1987. This applies irrespective of whether or not the employee intends to return to work after the confinement. For liability to arise the employee must satisfy three tests:

(1) She has been continuously employed with the employer for at least 26 weeks before the expected week of confinement (EWC);
(2) Her normal weekly earnings in the eight weeks preceding the 14th week before EWC are not less than the current lower earnings limit for national insurance contributions (£39 per week in 1987/88);
(3) She has reached the beginning of the 11th week before EWC (or has already been confined).

SMP is payable for a maximum period of 18 weeks, normally beginning with the 11th week before EWC. It may be terminated before the end of the 18-week period, for example if the employee starts work.

SMP is normally payable at a single rate of £32·85 per week. However, where the employee has worked for the employer for at least two years (five years in the case of a part-time employee) before EWC, a higher rate is applicable equivalent to nine-tenths of her normal weekly earnings.

As with SSP, employers can reclaim the gross amount of SMP from the monthly national insurance contributions that they are due to account for through the PAYE system. SMP is liable to PAYE and national insurance contributions. Employers are required to keep records of SMP payments for at least three years after the tax year to which they relate.

Here again, the DHSS have published a booklet (NI 257) on the subject.

5 Preparing for Retirement

Retirement is a long way into the future for David Wiltshire – why should he have to think about it at all? Obviously he cannot go into an occupational pension scheme as described in 4.4.6 as this is open only to employees; but it is possible for those individuals in self-employment or employees not in a pensionable employment to obtain tax relief in respect of premiums paid to secure a retirement annuity provided it is in a form approved by the Inland Revenue. It is also possible to claim relief on premiums paid to obtain an annuity for a widow or other dependent relatives.

In view of the effects of inflation, the sooner an individual in the position of David Wiltshire starts thinking about making provision for his pension the better.

5.1 RETIREMENT ANNUITIES

Where a pension is provided through, say, a company pension scheme, the final pension payable is usually related to the period over which contributions have been made and the final salary at normal retirement date. This is not the case with retirement annuities.

The benefits possible under these arrangements are effectively restricted in two ways. The first restriction is by the amount of maximum premiums which it is permitted can be paid into this type of policy. The maximum premiums are based on a percentage of *net relevant earnings* and the age of the person concerned at the time of the payment. 'Net relevant earnings' are relevant earnings from a business or non-pensionable employment less certain deductions such as expenses, trading losses and capital allowances. Personal deductions, such as mortgage interest, are not taken into account.

Up to 5 April 1987, the maximum percentages of net relevant earnings were as shown below:

Year of birth	*Percentage*
1934 or any later year	$17\frac{1}{2}$
1916 to 1933	20
1914 or 1915	21
1912 or 1913	24

From 6 April 1987, the percentages are based on the individual's age as follows:

Age	*Percentage*
Up to 50	$17\frac{1}{2}$
51–55	20

56–60	22½
61–75	27½

The other restriction is that by the very nature of these schemes all the contributions paid by a policy holder go into building up a cash fund. When normal retirement date is reached, as most policies have an *open market option*, the policy holder can go into the market and buy the best annuity possible at the time from whichever company is offering the best rates. However, the final pension payable is dependent upon the interest rate prevailing at the time of retirement. Interest rates have lately been prone to fairly major fluctuations and it is not anticipated in the short to medium term that this is likely to change, so the timing can be critical.

One alternative is for individuals to subscribe at least part of their total premium payments to a true deferred annuity contract. Under this type of arrangement each premium purchases a guaranteed amount of final pension to which, as time goes on, bonuses are added in much the same way as the traditional with-profit endowment policy. As with all bonus additions once these are given they cannot be taken away, and therefore policy holders are always aware of the minimum levels of final pension to which they can expect to become entitled. Because the insurance company concerned is having to provide a guaranteed minimum pension their projection of what this might be for a given investment is likely to be based on more conservative assumptions than might otherwise be the case.

The main benefits that can be enjoyed are as follows:

(1) *A retirement pension*. This can commence at a minimum
     age of 60 (50 for contracts taken out on or after
     4 January 1988), although for persons in certain
     occupations approval has been given for them to
     commence earlier; but the pension must be taken not
     later than at age seventy-five.
(2) Instead of a full pension, for contracts taken out on
     or after 4 January 1988 a *tax-free lump sum* of up to
     25% of the accumulated fund (subject to an overriding
     maximum of £150,000 per contract) may be taken at
     retirement.

     For contracts taken out prior to 4 January 1988 the
     limits are differently calculated as follows:

Date of contract	Normal maximum	Overriding maximum
Prior to 17 March 1987	Three times remaining pension after taking lump sum	Not applicable
Between 18 March 1987 and 3 January 1988 (both dates inclusive)	As above	£150,000 per contract

     Where a scheme does not allow for the 'open market
     option' described above to be taken it is advisable to

take the lump sum and purchase an annuity at the best rates possible in the market.

(3) On death before retirement a pension or lump sum can be provided for *a widow or dependants* by allocating up to 5% of net relevant earnings for this purpose. This has to come out of the maximum contributions of 17½% (or higher depending on age), so reducing the fund available for the contributor's own benefit.

(4) It may be possible for there to be an element of increase built into the pension payable.

(5) Usually, if the contributor dies before reaching normal retirement age, the pension contributions made will be returned, possibly with interest, but the amount recoverable cannot exceed the total value of the pension fund at the time of death.

Tax relief is effectively given on contributions made at the individual's highest income tax rate and there is a great measure of flexibility in how the premium can be used to reduce liabilities as far as possible.

An individual may pay a premium in one year of assessment and elect to have it related back to the previous year of assessment. Therefore, an individual has twelve months following the year of assessment in which relief will be given in which to ascertain the level of relevant earnings and pay the appropriate premiums. Where there are no relevant earnings in this preceding year of assessment, the individual may go back to the year before that. Although the premium must actually be paid in the year following that to which it is to relate, the claim for this treatment need not be sent to the Revenue until the following 5 July. To illustrate, if it is intended that a premium paid in 1987/88 be related back to 1986/87 the premium must be paid before 6 April 1988 and the election submitted by 5 July 1988.

It is also possible to review the position and ensure that, for each of the tax years up to seven years before the year in which the premium is paid, the maximum premiums possible have been paid and relief obtained. Thus, where the total amount of qualifying premiums paid in any one year is less than the amount on which relief could have been claimed, this *unused relief* may be carried forward and used up in any of the following six years of assessment. This relief is in addition to the normal 17½% (or more depending on age) rate of tax-deductible premiums payable, provided there are sufficient relevant earnings against which to set the relief. However, care should be taken that personal allowances, etc. are not lost by paying too much in any one year. Unused relief brought forward is dealt with on a 'first in, first out' basis and, therefore, if by the end of 1987/88 (bearing in mind that one can elect to carry premiums back to 1986/87) unused relief for 1980/81 has not been utilized it will be lost. One further important condition that must be met before previous years' unused premiums can be utilized is that in the year to which the premium payment is assigned, i.e. the year of payment or the previous year, the maximum permitted premium payments *for that year* must be paid up first.

It was previously a condition of obtaining Revenue approval of a contract, and thus obtaining relief on premiums paid, that lump sums or returns of premiums or interest on premiums or bonuses out of profits were to be payable only to an individual's personal representatives. This requirement has been withdrawn and these payments may now be made to any person. It is thus possible for contracts to be drawn up (or existing contracts to be amended) in conjunction with a form of trust so that these payments can be made outside the scope of inheritance tax.

Where a partner in a partnership is paying retirement annuity premiums and also pays annuities to former partners, the Revenue agree that in calculating the net relevant earnings of the paying partner a deduction for the annuity paid to the former partner is not needed. Such a payment is made for 'proprietorial' purposes rather than for the trade or profession and would be disallowed as they have not been wholly and exlusively incurred for the purposes of the business. The payment is in the nature of a personal charge on income which, like other such charges, does not need to be deducted in arriving at net relevant earnings, though they are deductible from the payer's total income for tax purposes. The treatment of these annuities is considered in more detail in 7.5.

5.2 LOAN BACK FACILITIES

It is now possible to obtain loans from either the pension company's funds or a banking arrangement which can be connected to the provision of a pension. One option is to follow the endowment route of borrowing funds from a bank or building society to purchase the borrower's main residence, with the proceeds from the policy, either on death or maturity, being payable to the lending institution and this being their security for the funds advanced to buy the property. However, when the mortgage is linked to a pension fund the interest only is payable as before but the capital is repaid out of the pension fund lump sum commutation (as mentioned in 5.1, a proportion of the fund may be applied in this way). Other reasons for which funds may be needed are in connection with school fees or the purchase of business properties.

However, remember that all policies of this type are non-assignable and therefore are not available to be used as security for a loan. Should there be insufficient assets which can be used as security the lender is merely recognizing the existence of the pension scheme, where there is an anticipated excess, and lending up to a certain limit which will represent a multiple of either the expected annual contribution or a percentage of the tax-free lump sum expected at retirement date. One condition that will be imposed upon the borrower is that the loan will become repayable should the pension contributions cease. Also, although the Chancellor has decided not to attack lump sums by taxing them for the present, this may not always be so and the impact that a charge to tax could have on the final net sum receivable might make this particular route for loan financing less sound.

5.3 SELF-INVESTED SCHEMES

Under this arrangement, which to a certain extent mirrors self-administered pension schemes for employees described in 4.4.6, the insurance company identifies contributions paid by a policy holder or a group of policy holders such as partners in a partnership. The fund is usually operated by an investment adviser nominated by the policy holder(s). Assets which can be used in the business, such as office or business premises, can be bought by the fund and then leased back to the policy holder(s). The benefit of arranging matters in this way is that any future capital growth in the value of the property will not be subject to capital gains tax nor will the rents received be subject to income tax because these gains are received by a tax-exempt fund. The rental payments will, of course, be tax deductible in calculating the taxable profits of the policy holder(s). With industrial buildings, as mentioned in 3.4, it is possible for a joint election to be made which allows the lessees to claim the IBAs available, thereby further reducing the tax liability of the policy holder(s). In this situation it is expected that the rental charge would be that much higher but overall an increased tax benefit should be possible.

It should always be remembered that the main purpose of the pension fund must be to provide a pension for the policy holder(s). The Superannuation Funds Office will not look benignly on a scheme which seems to be a mere adjunct of the main business, and therefore at all times transactions between the two must not only be commercial but must be seen to be so.

6 The Final Years

After a number of years of hard but also successful and profitable work running his business on his own, David Wiltshire is now considering a change of direction. This could take the form of disposing of the business and retiring, and the tax implications of this are considered in this chapter. There are also the possibilities of going into partnership, perhaps with his son Richard, and of incorporation, and these are looked at in Chapters 7 and 8.

6.1 WHEN DOES A BUSINESS CEASE?

As with the commencement it is a question of fact as to whether or not a business has ceased. It is very important to determine when a trade, profession or vocation has permanently discontinued because, as a general rule, expenses incurred after the date of cessation are not deductible in calculating profits, whereas post-cessation receipts still remain taxable.

A trade can be said to have permanently ceased if it is not

expected that any further sales will be made and no effort is made to secure further sales. It is important to distinguish between those sales which are connected with the closing down of the business and those sales which are the final throes of carrying on the trade. To illustrate, where normal trading stock is sold until such time as there is nothing left, there is a continuing trade which has not finally ceased until there is no stock left to sell. However, where the complete business is disposed of as a going concern this is not a trading transaction in itself and the business can be expected to have ceased at the close of trading by the old owner prior to the moment when the new owner takes over the business.

Specific difficulties may arise where the trader dies. As a general rule the deceased's personal representatives step into his or her shoes. They are likely to wish to realize the assets of the trade as soon as possible unless they have power to carry on the business and wish to do so. As to whether a trade is being carried on or merely the assets used in the trade are being disposed of will again be a question of fact.

6.2 POST-CESSATION RECEIPTS AND EXPENSES

Where a trade ceases generally all sums received on or after the date the trade was permanently discontinued are charged to tax under the rules of Schedule D Case VI. Tax is chargeable on the full amount of the receipts normally on a current year basis although a preceding year basis may be used where the source is likely to go on producing receipts for an extended period of time. Reasonable expenses are, in practice, usually allowable as are writing-down allowances (see Chapter 3).

The cost of redundancy payments or other types of employers' payments under the Employment Protection (Consolidation) Act 1978 are allowable. The maximum payments that can be made under these provisions are related to the salary paid to the employee, the employee's age and the period of time for which he has worked for the employer in a 'full-time' capacity: this is taken to be more than sixteen hours per week.

In addition to these statutory payments any additional employers' payments to employees whose contracts have been terminated on cessation of the business will be tax deductible and treated as having been made on the last day of trading. The maximum allowable additional payment is three times the statutory payment referred to above. Revenue practice is also to allow, as a deduction, such payments on a partial cessation, i.e. where an identifiable element of the total trading entity is permanently discontinued.

6.3 CLOSING YEARS' RULES OF ASSESSMENT

When a business permanently ceases special rules are applied in calculating the amount of profits assessable which are similar to those applied to the commencement basis. Where there is merely a temporary stoppage of trade these rules do not come into operation.

The assessment for the fiscal year ended 5 April in which

the business ceases is based on the profits of the period from the previous 6 April, the beginning of that fiscal year, to the date that the trade actually ceased. The two years prior to that year, the penultimate and pre-penultimate years of assessment, are initially assessed on the preceding year basis but the Revenue have the power to amend those assessments to the actual profits earned in those fiscal years. They are allowed to do this only where the total of the profits of those two years calculated on an actual basis exceed the profits of the two years calculated on the preceding year basis. These principles are applied only to the adjusted taxable profits of the business and take no account of capital allowances or personal reliefs, etc. These calculations should take into account the exact number of days that each accounting period runs in a particular tax year to ensure that the profit apportionments are precise.

Special rules also apply to the computation of capital allowances in these closing years.

EXAMPLE 9

David ceases trading on 30 September 1989 and his taxable profits for the years running up to that date are as follows:

Years ended 31 December 1985	£7,000
1986	£14,000
1987	£11,000
Year ended 31 December 1988	£20,000
9 months ended 30 September 1989	£6,000

The original assessments would be:

1986/87 PY – year ended 31 December 1985		£7,000
1987/88 PY – year ended 31 December 1986	14,000	
1988/89 PY – year ended 31 December 1987	11,000	
		£25,000

1989/90 actual 6 April to 30 September 1989	
178/273 days × £6,000	£3,912

If the Revenue take up their option to revise the assessments:

1986/87 PY – year to 31 December 1985		
As before		£7,000
1987/88 actual 6 April 1987 to 5 April 1988		
6 April to 31 December 1987		
270/365 × £11,000	8,137	
1 January to 5 April 1988		
96/366 × £20,000	5,246	
		13,383
1988/89 actual 6 April 1988 to 5 April 1989		
6 April to 31 December 1988		
270/366 × £20,000	14,754	
1 January to 5 April 1989		
95/273 × £6,000	2,088	
		16,842
		£30,225

1989/90 actual 6 April to 30 September 1989
     As before   £3,912

Therefore the Revenue would exercise their option so that aggregate profits of £30,225 would be assessed rather than £25,000.

6.4   LOSSES IN THE FINAL YEARS

Where a trade is permanently discontinued and a loss is sustained in the last twelve months for which the business was carried on, that loss may be carried back and set off against assessments on the business for the three years of assessment preceding the fiscal year in which cessation takes place, provided that relief in respect of the loss has not been given in any other way. The relief is set against profits for the penultimate year first and carried back until exhausted. This relief is available only to be given against profits arising in the same trade as that in which the loss was incurred.

Where it is decided that it is more tax efficient to set losses against other income arising in the year, care is necessary following a discontinuance of a business. Normally the Revenue apply the loss shown in the accounts to the particular fiscal year in which the accounting period ends but consider that, legally, losses should be apportioned over the fiscal year. This method is followed where a business ceases. Care is necessary because where a proportion of a loss is apportioned to the preceding tax year it may be disallowed because a claim has already been allowed for a

full year's loss in that preceding year; it may be then
necessary to reopen the position and request that the
apportionment rules be applied for all relevant tax years in
date, i.e. those falling within the last six years.

6.5   RETIREMENT RELIEF (CAPITAL GAINS TAX)

This is a very useful relief which is available to be set against
the capital gain arising on the disposal of a business. This
can include the disposal of an interest in a partnership or of
shares in a family trading company; for convenience the
particular provisions relating to these other types of business
vehicle are looked at here. The disposal of part of a business
may also qualify for relief.

The main conditions which need to be satisfied before
retirement relief is available are:

(1)   The individual must have reached the age of sixty years
or be retiring early through ill-health; *and*
(2)   He must be disposing of the whole or part of a business
which he owns or of shares in a family trading company
of which he is a full-time working director.

The maximum relief amounting to £125,000 (£100,000 up
to 5 April 1987) is available where the second condition
mentioned above is satisfied throughout a period of ten
years ending with the disposal. Although strictly the individual must have carried on the business or been a full-time
working director throughout the ten years to comply, relief

will still be available where separate businesses are owned in succession. The ten-year rule is also regarded as satisfied where initially the individual carries on the trade personally and subsequently becomes a full-time director of a family company which takes over the trade.

Where the ten-year requirement is not met the relief is reduced on a percentage scale dropping from 100% for ten years to 10% for one year. These conditions must be satisfied for at least one year for any relief to be available.

EXAMPLE 10

David is aged sixty-three when he disposes of his business realizing a chargeable gain of £100,000; he has been carrying on the business for six years. His entitlement to retirement relief is restricted to 6/10 of £125,000 i.e. £75,000, leaving £25,000 still chargeable to tax (subject to any annual exemption).

In contrast to the position where the directors of a family company have to be occupied full-time in carrying on the business, an individual does not need to have been engaged full-time to qualify for relief.

Where an asset is owned by an individual and has been used by a firm in which he is a partner, retirement relief may be due where the individual has made the property available rent free or has not charged a full market rent, although in the latter situation the relief will be restricted to represent the proportionate shortfall. In this situation it is better not to charge rent but to seek an appropriate adjustment to the firm's profit sharing ratios so that an amount equivalent to the rent is received.

Where a property is owned jointly by a husband and wife and only one of them carries on a business, only that person will receive retirement relief as the other is not carrying on a business and is therefore not entitled.

As mentioned above, where particular individuals are full-time working directors, relief will be available where they dispose of shares in a family trading company. A family trading company is one where the individual concerned can exercise at least 25% of the voting rights or where he owns at least 5% himself and his family more than 50%. 'Family' in this context means the individual's spouse, and any brother, sister, ancestor or descendant of the individual or his spouse. Full-time working directors are defined as those who are required to devote substantially the whole of their time to the service of the company in a managerial or technical capacity. This definition must be approached with some care because in one case the courts decided that a woman director who worked at least three full days per week, and occasionally more, was not a full-time director. The test generally accepted for other tax purposes seems to be a minimum of twenty-five hours per week.

Where both husband and wife are directors of the company, for each to qualify for relief it is important that they are both full-time working directors and they both hold at least 5% of the voting shares each in their own names. If only one spouse qualifies and meets both ten-year and share requirements, and the other spouse does not although he holds say 85% of the company's shares, the latter spouse can transfer those shares to the former who then disposes of them and utilizes the maximum retirement relief available.

Where properties are used by the family trading company in order to obtain retirement relief, broadly the same requirements must be met. However, there is one distinct difference in that the disposal of such assets must be associated with a disposal of shares in that company by the director to qualify for relief. Relief will not be available where the property used by the company is disposed of but the director retains his shares.

There is a further possible restriction of the relief which can trap the unwary. The relief is restricted to a maximum proportion of the gain arising on *chargeable business assets*. These are assets used for the purposes of the trade carried on by individuals or their family trading company and are those assets which if disposed of would produce a gain chargeable to capital gains tax as opposed to income tax. Included here would be goodwill and freehold premises but not stock or debtors. Where the shares in a family trading company are disposed of, the following fraction is applied to the chargeable gain arising on the shares:

$$\frac{\text{chargeable business assets}}{\text{total chargeable assets}}$$

Where a company retains investments, which are chargeable but not business assets, this will have the effect of reducing the amount of relief available by their proportion to total chargeable assets. Therefore, prior to a disposal it may be advisable to dispose of those assets and retain cash which is not a chargeable asset.

EXAMPLE 11

In March 2002 David sells his shares in Wiltshire Enterprises Ltd realizing a capital gain of £100,000. As he is
sixty-three and meets all the other requirements this
would normally be covered by retirement relief. The
company's balance sheet shows its assets at current values
to be as follows:

	£
Freehold premises	200,000
Stocks and shares	50,000
Cash	25,000
	£275,000

The maximum relief to which David would be entitled
would be:

$$\frac{\text{chargeable business assets}}{\text{total chargeable assets}} = \frac{200,000}{250,000} \times 100,000 = \underline{\underline{£80,000}}$$

However, should the stocks and shares be sold for cash
the whole gain attributable to the business would be
exempt as the chargeable business assets would be the
same as the total business assets and there would be no
restriction. Of course any gains realized by the business
on this disposal would be chargeable in the usual way.

6.6 DEREGISTRATION FOR VAT PURPOSES

When traders are deregistered they are deemed to have
disposed of their business assets which would include plant

and trading stock and therefore to have made a supply for VAT purposes. The tax payable is calculated by reference to the cost of the assets. However, where particular items did not qualify for an input tax credit or if the total output tax on the remaining items would not exceed a total of £250 no charge arises.

Where a business is disposed of as a going concern for VAT purposes this is deemed to be a supply made in the course or furtherance of the business. In these circumstances all the assets are chargeable to tax, but there are exceptions to this rule as follows:

(1) Provided the business is transferred before the transferor's registration is cancelled and the person acquiring the business will in consequence of this acquisition become a taxable person and intends to carry on the same kind of business the supply is treated as being outside the scope of these provisions.

(2) Where the business is transferred to a taxable person no liability to output tax will arise and the deemed supply of the business assets at the date of deregistration is ignored.

In these circumstances where the transferor is ceasing business altogether and the transferee is becoming newly registered as a result of the transfer, it is possible to arrange for the VAT registration number to be transferred with the business. This is convenient where it is desired to retain continuity, but it should be noted that the transferee takes over the continuing liability to make returns, and to deal with claims and disputes with Customs and any other such matters relating to the transferor.

7 The Business Partnership

David Wiltshire is approached by some people who want to go into partnership with him. He is also thinking of bringing his son Richard into the business as a partner.

7.1 DEFINITION OF A PARTNERSHIP

The legal definition of a partnership is:

> 'The relationship which subsists between persons carrying on a business in common and with a view to profit.'

Although under English law (but not under Scottish law), a partnership is not a legal entity with an existence in its own right, unlike a company, whilst a person is a partner he is jointly liable for all the debts and obligations of the firm. Thus a partnership is something not to be entered into lightly and in some respects is akin to marriage.

7.2 ASSESSMENT FOR TAX PURPOSES

7.2.1 Normal basis

Although not necessarily a separate legal entity, for convenience the partnership is treated as a separate body for income tax purposes. Therefore individual assessments are not raised on each partner but a joint assessment is raised on the partnership as a whole. Each partner is jointly liable to pay the tax liability calculated in the assessment, but attached to it will be a schedule which will show the individual tax liability of each partner and usually each partner will contribute to meet his share accordingly. In arriving at this liability the usual deductions and personal allowances are given and each partner is, of course, entitled to his own range of basic and higher rate tax bands.

In common with all assessments to tax on trading profits under Schedule D, the tax liability will be due in two instalments on 1 January in the year of assessment and on the following 1 July. In the normal way this assessment is based on the profits of the accounting period ending in the previous year of assessment. The profits of a partnership are apportioned in accordance with the agreed profit-sharing ratios of that year of assessment and not that applying in the accounting period or the year of assessment in which that period ends.

EXAMPLE 12

David, George and Andrew are in partnership, making up their accounts to 31 March each year. The accounts to

31 March 1987 show a taxable profit (assessable under the preceding year rules in 1987/88) of £36,000, which it has been agreed should be shared equally between them.

For the year ended 31 March 1988, the partners agree that in recognition of David's particular efforts on behalf of the firm they will now share profits as to David one-half and George and Andrew one-quarter each.

The income tax assessment for 1987/88 will also be divided on this amended basis, thus –

	£
David	18,000
George	9,000
Andrew	9,000
	£36,000

– even though the underlying profits were divided equally.

Note that partners' salaries and interest on capital are *not* allowable expenses for tax purposes, being regarded as a part of the partnership profits and an ingredient in the method of dividing them between the partners.

7.2.2   On a change of partner

The commencing rules, as described in 2.4, apply with some modifications where there is a change in the membership of the partnership, e.g. a new member is admitted or an existing member retires or dies. Under these circumstances there is a cessation of the 'old' partnership and the commencement of a 'new' one. The closing year rules of Schedule D are applied to the old partnership as set out in 6.3 while modified opening year rules apply to the profits of the new partnership even though the business continues to trade in the normal way.

The *modified commencement rules* were introduced with effect from 19 March 1985, as it previously had been possible for a partnership to reduce its overall tax charge quite substantially by organizing a change in its membership at the most appropriate moment. Where the election described below is not made, the new partnership will be assessed for each of the first four years on the actual profits arising in those years and the previous year basis will apply for the fifth and subsequent years of assessment. In the fifth and sixth years an option to have the profits of both years assessed on an actual basis is available.

These new rules do *not* apply where a sole trader such as David Wiltshire takes in one or more partners, nor where a partnership is dissolved so that only one individual remains to carry on the business on his own. In these situations the normal assessment rules described in 2.4 apply unchanged.

However, it is recognized that the opening and closing year rules may be inequitable and subject to certain conditions being met an election can be made so that both the old and new partnerships are treated as if they had been continuing and assessments will be raised on the new firm on the normal preceding year basis. As described above, the profits will be apportioned between the old and new partnerships for the fiscal year in which the change takes place. The election must be made in writing and signed by

all the partners of both the old and new firms and sent to
the Revenue within two years of the date of the change.
Where the change is brought about because a partner has
died his personal representatives must sign. There must also
be at least one partner who was a member of both the old
and the new partnerships. If an election is made and it is
later decided that this was a mistake it can be revoked within
two years of the date of the change.

Special considerations apply where two partnerships
merge or where a relatively large firm absorbs a much
smaller one so that its business loses its identity.

It is likely when considering whether a continuation
election should be submitted or not that certain partners will
gain and others will lose. It is usual practice for the majority
who gain, whichever course of action is followed, to be
allowed to do so upon giving indemnities to those who may
have to find further tax.

7.2.3   Capital allowances

Where the partnership ceases under these circumstances a
notional sale of plant and machinery and buildings at full
market value will arise. There are certain disadvantages in
this happening.

First, there is likely to be a (perhaps substantial) balancing
charge on the old partnership. Secondly, it will be possible
to claim only writing-down allowances on the assets taken
over by the new partnership, and these are likely to be
considerably less than the balancing charge already mentioned.

However, on the footing that the partners in the old firm

and the partners in the new firm are 'connected' persons for tax purposes, it is possible to submit an election to the Revenue to the effect that there is a continuity of the trade for the purposes of claiming capital allowances. In effect the new firm picks up the allowance where the old firm finishes and there is no balancing charge on the transfer.

Where a partner owns plant and machinery in his own right and it is not regarded as a partnership asset, he may allow the partnership to use that plant for no consideration. The partnership is able to claim allowances in respect of the cost of the plant as though it had belonged to the partnership but, in practice, the benefit of those allowances usually goes to the partner who incurred the expenditure. The effect of this is that any allowances due will normally be set against the partner's share of profit in the appropriate year of assessment and any excess can be set against his other general income. Where one partner has substantial income which arises outside the partnership this may be quite a tax-efficient way of organizing the purchase of plant and machinery. However, one disadvantage is that VAT paid on the purchase that might normally be reclaimed will not be recoverable.

7.2.4   Work in progress

The profits of a business for taxation purposes are normally calculated on an 'earnings' basis, that is to say including all credits and liabilities accruing during the period covered by the accounts: thus there will be included a figure for work in progress. This may be calculated in a number of different ways depending on the nature of the firm's business but each item or subject being valued at *the lower of cost and net realizable value*. This will normally exclude any element of profit, in particular anything for partners' time. An exception to this is for long-term contracts in the construction industry where it may be appropriate to recognize a part of the accrued profit prior to completion.

In some cases, notably professional partnerships, profits are calculated on some other basis generally referred to as a *conventional* basis. They include those cases where no account is taken of work in progress so that profit is calculated by reference to bills rendered or even in some cases to cash receipts and payments only. The use of such bases goes back to the time when accounting records were less sophisticated than they are now, especially with the use of computers, and the evaluation of work in progress was correspondingly more difficult.

A conventional basis of calculating profits is likely to be advantageous particularly in a time of inflation and rising profits because it will result in a deferral of profit and thus taxation. It should not be surrendered without careful consideration.

On a cessation the Revenue will require closing work in progress to be brought into account. Furthermore following a cessation the Revenue will require the new firm to be assessed on a full earnings basis for at least the first three years. In practice it is most unlikely that the Revenue will agree to a business now on an earnings basis changing to a conventional basis.

Apart from a straightforward transfer at valuation as determined above, there are various ways of dealing with work in progress on the cessation of a partnership. It may be left with the old partnership to realize in the succeeding accounting periods. In this case the new firm may assist with the realization and charge a fee for its services. One consequence of this arrangement will be that the new firm starts with no work in progress at all. Since a significant proportion of fees charged and cash received in the period after the cessation will be in respect of the old firm's work in progress, there will be a proportionately lower profit in the new firm. The profit on the old firm's work in progress will be assessed separately on the partners concerned on an actual basis under the rules of Schedule D Case VI as described in 6.2.

Another alternative is for the old firm to sell the work in progress at the date of cessation to the new firm at a fair market price which might include partners' salaries. Again a significant part of the billing and receipts in the first accounting period of the new firm will relate to its work in progress. At the end of its first accounting period the new firm would revert to the more usual conservative basis of valuation of its work in progress, i.e. salary costs with nothing included for partners' time or overheads. For tax purposes the result will be much as before. A significant part of the first year's income would relate to the old firm's work in progress with the result that the new firm's profit would be lower.

7.2.5 Partnership losses

Where a partnership makes a loss for tax purposes, in principle the reliefs as described in 2.6 and 6.4 are available. However all the partners can decide separately, having regard to their personal circumstances, which of the various options they will use for their share of the loss.

As with profits, the loss is allocated between partners in the profit-sharing ratio applicable to the year of assessment in which the loss is recognized for tax purposes, which may not necessarily be the same as the period for which the accounts are made up. In particular this allocation may be affected by the way in which individual partners take up the relief.

EXAMPLE 13

Derek, John and Clive operate in partnership and share profits and losses in the ratio 45:30:25, but from 30 June 1987 this is changed to 2:2:1. For the year ended 31 December 1987 a loss of £10,000, adjusted for tax purposes, is made.

(a) If the loss is to be relieved in 1987/88 it is allocated as follows:

Apportionment of loss

6 April – 30 June 1987	3/12 × £10,000	£2,500
1 July 1987 – 5 April 1988	9/12 × £10,000	£7,500

Allocation

	Total £	Derek £	John £	Clive £
6 April– 30 June 1987				
45 : 30 : 25	2,500	1,125	750	625

	Total £	Derek £	John £	Clive £
1 July 1987– 5 April 1988				
2 : 2 : 1	7,500	3,000	3,000	1,500
	£10,000	£4,125	£3,750	£2,125

(b) If the loss is to be carried forward to 1988/89 or later years the allocation is made as follows:

Apportionment of loss
1 January–30 June 1987   6/12×£10,000 £5,000
1 July–31 December 1987   6/12×£10,000 £5,000

Allocation

	Total £	Derek £	John £	Clive £
1 January– 30 June 1987				
45 : 30 : 25	5,000	2,250	1,500	1,250
Forward	5,000	2,250	1,500	1,250
1 July– 31 December 1987				
2 : 2 : 1	5,000	2,000	2,000	1,000
	£10,000	£4,250	£3,500	£2,250

It is open to Derek and Clive for example to carry their losses forward whereas John could decide to relieve his loss in the year. This would result in the total of £10,250 (i.e. £4,250 + £3,750 + £2,250) being relieved instead of the actual loss of £10,000.

7.3   INVESTMENT INCOME

Other income that may form part of the income of the partnership could include income from property, taxed interest such as bank interest arising in the UK and any untaxed income arising from abroad. In the normal way this income will be included in the accounts, but in arriving at the profit chargeable to tax under Schedule D it is added back and allocated separately amongst the partners. As this income is not earned income it cannot be included in calculating net relevant earnings for retirement annuity premium relief purposes (see 5.1).

The income is allocated to fiscal years in the same way as applies to earned income in that the income is allocated in accordance with the profit-sharing ratio of a particular fiscal year; if there is a change in that ratio during the year the income is apportioned on a time basis and allocated to the profit-sharing ratio operating in each period to arrive at the total chargeable for the tax year. The allocation of income does not affect the normal rules of assessment relating to different types of income.

7.4   ANNUAL CHARGES

Partnership annual charges must be paid under deduction of income tax at the basic rate (currently 27%). They are added back in calculating the taxable profits of the partnership, but each partner does get relief for these as a deduction from his total income for that tax year, his share being arrived at using the profit-sharing ratio for the fiscal year concerned. One difference here though is that where there is a change in profit-sharing ratio or a change in the members carrying on the partnership in the tax year the charges are allocated to the periods before and after the change in accordance with the amounts actually *paid* in each particular period.

7.5 ANNUITIES

Payment of annuities to former partners or their dependants is becoming less common than it was, partly because the continuing partners regard such annuities as millstones and partly because a retiring partner may be concerned at the ability of his younger colleagues to be able to keep up the payments. Certainly, where the partnership runs into difficulties and there are new partners who do not know the retired partner, this difficulty can be exacerbated. Nevertheless it may be easier for the continuing members to discharge the outgoing partner's share of goodwill by paying him an annuity than to raise a loan so that this can be done in one lump sum.

Partnership annuities are not retirement annuities as described in 5.1. With partnership annuities there is no element of insurance or of savings but they are paid on a pay-as-you go basis directed by the provisions in the partnership deed. They are in effect similar to national insurance retirement pensions paid by the government from current year national insurance contributions. However, one disadvantage is that the benefits arising under a partnership annuity are unsecured, in that they depend on personal covenants made by the continuing partners, whereas the benefits from a retirement annuity are secured by asset backing. The greatest benefit that can arise from the use of partnership annuities is that the impact that capital gains tax and inheritance tax have on partnership changes can be substantially mitigated. However, this would be of no comfort if, because of a later downturn in the fortunes of the business, there was no money actually to pay the annuity.

The main advantages are that, for the continuing partners, the payments made will qualify for tax relief at their highest rates of tax; they will not be considered to be making a settlement which has its own technical difficulties; and the payments that are made will not be considered to be a repayment of capital introduced or created by the retired partner.

One particular disadvantage is that the continuing partners may wish to limit the life of the annuity to a fixed term, say not more than ten years. This can lead to possible embarrassment if particular retired partners or their dependants find themselves in financial difficulties without the annuity.

7.6 TAX RELIEF ON BORROWING

Where money is borrowed by a working partner which is used to purchase a share in a partnership or to provide capital as a loan to the partnership, interest paid is a deductible expense. Care should be taken, however, in organizing matters so that relief is obtained or retained. For instance, if a partner has an excessive credit balance on his or her current account and wishes to use those funds to purchase a new house, but those funds are at the same time needed to finance the partnership, relief will not be forthcoming under this heading if money is borrowed from the bank and put into the partnership and then, later, capital is taken out to purchase the house. The correct way of organizing such a transaction would be for the partner to withdraw his capital first and then a short time later to borrow money from his bank or some other external source to provide working capital for the partnership (effectively but not explicitly replacing the cash recently withdrawn).

As a general rule, borrowing through the partnership reduces the profits of the current year but not necessarily those profits taxable in the year, whereas borrowing outside the partnership to buy into or lend capital to it reduces taxable income on a current year basis. Perhaps the best approach is to borrow inside the partnership for the first twelve months to keep profits as low as possible and thereafter outside to retain total flexibility. However, always be careful to follow the principles set out above when withdrawing capital and arranging new loans.

7.7 PARTNERSHIP AGREEMENTS

When creating a partnership it is advisable from the outset to have a partnership agreement which sets out the terms and arrangements under which the partnership is operated and the particular interests and rights of the partners carrying on the business. It is strongly recommended that the agreement should be in writing; while it is not essential to have it drawn up as a formal legal document, this is preferable in case of some subsequent dispute over its terms.

The main aspects that may be covered might be as follows:

(1) The basis of division of profits and losses, both revenue and capital, between the partners.
(2) The amount of capital that should be provided by each partner.
(3) The creation of tax reserves.
(4) The conditions under which capital or loan accounts are to be paid in or withdrawn.
(5) The payment of interest on capital and loan account balances.
(6) Partnership business premises – whether these should be owned by the individuals and leased to the partnership under a tenancy agreement, or be owned by the partnership. In the former situation to ensure that the partner(s) concerned are not put at a disadvantage a salary can be paid to them to compensate them for the rental forgone.
(7) Goodwill – whether a partner's share in the goodwill

of the business should be bought out when that partner leaves, or whether it is to accrue to the firm.

(8) Annuities – details of the circumstances under which annuities may become payable.

(9) Long-term sickness arrangements.

(10) Retirement from, and dissolution of, the partnership – this would cover the terms and conditions under which partners may be required to retire from the partnership and the way in which amounts credited to current or capital accounts may be paid out, i.e. by instalments with interest or in full. This would also cover any indemnities necessary and how to deal with retiring partners' tax liabilities. It may also be necessary to introduce restrictive covenants so as to ensure that the partner does not take work away from the partnership.

(11) Any requirements to be a signatory to partnership elections and related indemnities.

7.8 SALARIED PARTNERS

It is sometimes considered appropriate, rather than to make an individual a full profit-sharing partner (commonly referred to as an 'equity' partner), to pay him an enhanced salary, possibly combined with some profit-sharing element, in recognition of his senior status in the firm. Although the individual may be shown on the firm's notepaper as a partner, he would not be subject to the burden of unlimited liability for the firm's debts and would normally be given an indemnity by the other equity partners for this.

This is often a useful arrangement where it is intended to admit an individual to partnership but where, for commercial or tax reasons, it may not be appropriate to do so at a particular time.

For tax purposes a salaried partner will normally be treated as an employee taxable under Schedule E and he will not share in the partnership taxable profits or losses. His appointment as a salaried partner will not of itself constitute a partnership change with the consequences described in 7.2.2, but his subsequent admission as an equity partner would.

Alternatively, if the individual does share in the partnership profits or losses, while still receiving the larger part of his 'reward' from the firm by way of a fixed 'salary', he would then be taxable under Schedule D through the usual machinery of the partnership assessment. He would also be liable to Class 2 and 4 national insurance contributions, which could show a substantial saving compared with the Class 1 contributions due for him as an employee (see 1.3, 4.4.10 and Appendix C).

7.9 VALUE ADDED TAX

For VAT purposes the partnership is treated as continuing where a partner retires or a new partner is admitted, provided that the firm continues to exist. Where the partnership is dissolved, however, deregistration will follow even if a former partner becomes a sole trader. Customs and Excise should be notified of any admissions or retirement of partners within twenty-one days of the event. This is particularly important from the retired partner's point of view, because he remains jointly liable for the firm's VAT liability arising between the date of his retirement and the date that the authorities are notified of this event.

7.10 CAPITAL TAX ASPECTS AND TAX PLANNING

7.10.1 Inheritance tax

The notes which follow are concerned with the new *inheritance tax* (broadly a tax on asssets passing at death and on lifetime gifts made between individuals within seven years before the donor's death) which was introduced in the Budget of 18 March 1986 to replace the earlier *capital transfer tax*. Transactions of the kind described below that took place earlier may be within the scope of the former tax regime, and professional advice should be taken without delay. Further information on inheritance tax is given in 8.4.

The creation of a partnership offers important tax planning opportunities although caution is necessary. If, on the creation of the partnership, the benefits derived and the responsibilities of the partners are not commensurate with the value that they introduce into the partnership a transfer of value may occur, giving rise to a potential liability to inheritance tax, if a transferor dies within seven years (this is generally referred to as a *potentially exempt transfer*). Where partners are related to each other it is necessary to show that there was no gratuitous intent and also that the initial terms of the partnership are such as might be expected to be made between unconnected persons dealing at arm's length. Where the persons who are entering into partnership are unconnected prior to becoming partners, a claim that there was no intention to confer gratuitous intent should be accepted without difficulty.

Where a new partnership is created with, perhaps, the addition of a son to his parents' partnership, and it is intended that the partnership will hold valuable assets for the purposes of its trade, it is possible to undertake a fairly simple *estate freezing* exercise. For example, if on the creation of the partnership the husband and wife introduce a property worth £500,000 equally between them the sum of £250,000 will be credited to each of their capital accounts. To the extent that any of this value is transferred to the son a chargeable transfer will be considered to have taken place, in that it is unusual to give away a slice of valuable assets to an *unconnected* person in this way. The partnership agreement can provide that all future capital profits should be shared between father, mother and son in the ratio of, say, 1 : 1 : 8. No transfer of value takes place on the creation of the partnership in this particular situation because what is effectively being given away is the *future* growth in the value of the asset.

Once this arrangement has been carried out, any variation in the capital profits ratio will constitute a potentially exempt transfer, leading to a liability to tax if the transferor dies within seven years.

Where a partner dies in harness, his or her interest in the

partnership (subject to a deduction for business property relief; see below) will have to be included in the assets passing on his or her death for inheritance tax purposes.

Normally, *50% business property relief* is available in respect of the transfer of a partner's share in a business so that only one-half of the value of the interest is potentially chargeable. However, where under the terms of the partnership agreement that interest must pass to the other partners so that there is effectively a binding contract for the disposal of the interest, no business property relief will be available. This relief can be substantial and therefore care must be taken in drafting partnership agreements. This problem can normally be overcome by providing that the transfer of a retiring partner's interest is covered by suitable options.

Where a partner allows the partnership to use land, buildings, machinery and plant owned by him in the business, he will normally be able to claim business property relief at *30%* of the value of those assets.

7.10.2   Capital gains tax

For capital gains tax purposes each partner is regarded as owning a fractional share of partnership assets, and tax in respect of chargeable gains accruing to the partners on the disposal of partnership assets is assessed and charged on them separately. There can be no partnership gain or partnership loss as such. Each partner computes his own gain or loss by reference to his interest in the partnership assets. Once computed, this gain or loss is aggregated with other personal gains or losses. It is therefore necessary for an individual to take account of partnership gains when making calculations to ensure that best possible use is made of his annual exemption (£6,600 for 1987/88).

A change in profit-sharing ratios, whereby individual partners' shares in the partnership assets change, will not result in a capital gains tax charge unless there are payments passing between partners. Thus where no adjustment is made through the partnership accounts (by revaluation of the assets, coupled with a corresponding increase or decrease in any partner's current or capital account at some date between the partner's acquisition and the change in his share) or separate financial arrangements are entered into, there will be no capital gains tax consequences. However, a partner whose share increases will carry forward a larger proportion of cost, and vice versa for a partner taking a reduced share.

Sharing of capital gains and losses in a partnership need not necessarily be in the same ratios as the sharing of profits. For example, it may be beneficial for one or a group of partners to provide capital funds for the purchase of a fixed asset such as a property. The partnership agreement might then provide that those partners should be entitled to the capital gain or increase in value of that property. It will be necessary to recompense them for providing the asset perhaps by paying them a rent or by allowing interest on the capital provided or by increasing their profit shares.

Care should be taken with goodwill in a partnership; with a view to mitigating capital gains tax ideally it should accrue automatically to the firm without payment, thus ensuring no liability to capital gains tax on retirement of a partner or change in profit-sharing ratios. Where a partner has paid for goodwill in the past and has now given up his entitlement, he may be able to obtain loss relief for capital gains tax.

The operation of *retirement relief* is described in 6.5.

7.10.3 Practical effect of variation of terms of partnership agreement

Where a partner's estate for inheritance tax purposes is reduced in value due to a change in the capital profit-sharing ratios, either when a new partner is introduced or under a rearrangement as has been mentioned above, a charge to inheritance tax may arise unless it can be shown that the arrangements are commercial.

EXAMPLE 14

The assets in David's business are as follows:

	£	Book value £	Market value £
Fixed assets			
business premises, at cost		100,000	250,000
plant and machinery,			
at cost	80,000		
depreciation	40,000		
		40,000	50,000

motor vehicles, at cost	15,000	
depreciation	5,000	
	———	
	10,000	10,000
	———	———
	150,000	310,000
Net current assets	10,000	10,000
(debtors, prepayments,		
etc. less liabilities)		
	———	———
	£160,000	£320,000

If David now brings Richard into partnership, say on equal shares, there can be both inheritance tax and capital gains tax implications. If Richard immediately acquires a half-share in the assets, there would be a potentially exempt transfer for *inheritance tax* purposes arrived at as follows:

	£	£
Market value of David's estate before Richard introduced into partnership		320,000
David's estate after partnership commences:		
capital account	160,000	
half-interest in undervalue of assets 1/2 (£320,000–£160,000)	80,000	
	———	
		240,000
		———

Reduction in estate	80,000
Less: Business property relief at 50%	40,000
Potentially exempt transfer	£40,000

Assuming that David now survives seven years, no inheritance tax would be due and this would be a useful way of transferring wealth to the next generation. However, if the risk of tax being payable was considered too great, David should consider retaining the business premises in his sole ownership so that all the inheritance tax and capital gains tax problems would be avoided. Each situation must, of course, be considered separately after taking into account the views of the individuals concerned. In many cases it may be preferable to transfer appreciating assets to the next generation now rather than waiting and incurring perhaps substantial liabilities later.

In any event, this charge can be reduced or avoided by using the 'estate freezing' concept described in 7.10.1, so that Richard becomes entitled to the larger part of the future capital growth in the value of the partnership assets.

Looking now at *capital gains tax*, if the assets are revalued so that the present uplift in their value is credited to the partners equally. David will be assessed to tax on the business premises only as follows:

	£	£
Disposal of half-interest in business premises		125,000
Cost of half-interest	50,000	

Plus indexation
allowance – say   5,000
                                            ————   55,000
                                                        ————
                                                      £70,000
                                                        ====

No charge to capital gains tax arises on the plant and
machinery or on the motor vehicles as their market value is
less than their cost (in any case *motor cars* are exempt from
the charge).

It will not be possible to hold over the tax charge here as
David will be deemed to have received consideration for this
disposal.

If the assets are *not* revalued, although the capital gain
arising from the deemed disposal of the business premises
would be the same, an election for the tax chargeable on the
gain to be held over would be possible.

There may be certain situations where the gratuitous
transfer of an interest in goodwill need not necessarily lead
to a potential inheritance tax liability. In the situation where
there is an intended transfer of value from older to younger
partners it may be possible to avoid a tax liability by showing
that the younger partners are taking on more and more
responsibility from older partners and that it is commercially
proper for them to receive a share of the older partners'
interest in the partnership. Under the terms of the partnership agreement it may be specified that a senior partner
need spend only as much time on partnership affairs as he
thinks fit and need not restrict himself to those affairs,
whereas the younger partners may be required to devote

the whole of their time to partnership matters and not be allowed to have any outside business interests. Where goodwill passes on the death or retirement of a senior partner to the younger partners without monetary payment the younger partners can claim to have provided consideration for the extra share of goodwill during the senior partner's time in the firm.

8   And Co. Ltd

The business has now been going for some time. David is aware that many of his business associates are running what is effectively their own business through a limited company and he wonders whether the time has come for him to incorporate.

This is a question of fundamental importance and is of course one that also needs to be considered when a business is first set up as well as at later stages in its development. Before dealing with specific taxation aspects, the other considerations that enter into this review are set out below.

8.1   ADVANTAGES AND DISADVANTAGES OF CORPORATE STRUCTURE

8.1.1   Limited liability

One of the major advantages of incorporation is the concept of *limited liability*. This can enable business people to separate their private and business activities and to limit their liability to the extent of funds contributed either by way of share capital or loan. This is certainly more advantageous than carrying on a business as a sole trader or in partnership, as in those situations the proprietors' liability is unlimited. Where the business is in a high risk area, such as in the new technology or services fields, a company structure is likely to prove more advantageous.

However, it is probable that the protection of limited liability may not be complete. Although it will be possible to protect oneself against trade creditors, most banks and lending institutions will usually require personal guarantees from directors/shareholders before they will lend to the company. Moreover, where a business is incorporated the proprietors will not be absolved from personal liability for debts incurred prior to incorporation.

8.1.2 Borrowing and attracting finance

It is usually easier for a company to obtain additional finance from bankers and lending institutions because it is possible for them to take a floating charge over the assets of the business. As mentioned before, this should be approached with care because it may restrict the future growth of the business. It is also possible that suppliers will give extended credit to a company whereas they might not to an individual because they feel that the company has a measure of permanence and is likely to prove more reliable.

A company also has opportunities not available to an individual or a partnership in raising further equity capital by using the *business expansion scheme* ('BES'). The terms and conditions of the scheme are complex but essentially its main features are as follows:

(1) *For the investor*
- (a) An individual who must be UK resident.
- (b) Tax relief is available up to the individual's highest rate of income tax – now a maximum of 60%.
- (c) The maximum annual investment is £40,000 with a minimum limit of £500.
- (d) With effect from 6 April 1987, up to one half of the amount invested in period 6 April to 5 October, subject to a limit of £5,000, may be carried back for relief in the preceding tax year (provided the £40,000 limit mentioned in (c) is not thereby exceeded).
- (e) Relief is available only in respect of ordinary shares which have no special rights and which must be held for at least five years.
- (f) Relief is available only for genuine investment and is withdrawn in whole or in part if the investor withdraws his money from the company or sells his shares within a five-year period or breaks some other condition of the scheme.
- (g) The scheme is for outside minority investors rather than people putting money into their own businesses. Relief will not be given where the individual (including his associates) owns more than 30% of the shares. An associate for this purpose includes husband, wife, parent or remoter forebear, child or remoter issue but *not* brother or sister.

(h)   An investor must not become a *paid* director of the company.

(2) *For the company*

(a)   It must be incorporated in the UK.

(b)   It must be resident in the UK and not resident elsewhere.

(c)   It must be an unquoted company, i.e. its shares must not be dealt in on The Stock Exchange or the Unlisted Securities Market but it may be dealt in on any other market; for example, on one of the over-the-counter markets or under rule 535(2) of The Stock Exchange.

(d)   It must have all its issued ordinary share capital fully paid up. The shares should carry no preferential rights to dividends, to assets on a winding up or to redemption.

(e)   It must not control another company, except a qualifying subsidiary, or be controlled by another company. A company may have subsidiaries but they must be at least 90% owned by the parent company and, with certain exceptions, must themselves all be qualifying companies.

(f)   It must not be controlled by an individual who also controls another company carrying on a similar trade.

(g)   The group must carry on its trading activities wholly or mainly in the UK. This does not prevent the company exporting some or even all of its output to an overseas country, provided the bulk of its activities are in fact carried on in the UK.

(h) Most conventional trading companies qualify except:

   (i) Those dealing in commodities, shares, securities, land and futures.

   (ii) Those dealing in goods other than in the course of an 'ordinary trade of wholesale or retail distribution' and within the latter category goods of a kind which are collected or held as investments if the company does not actively try to sell them. This could apply to investment articles such as fine wines and antiques.

   (iii) Those offering financial and related services.

   (iv) Those with high asset backing, where the value of the company's land and buildings is more than half its net assets.

For shares issued under the scheme on or before 18 March 1986, capital gains tax is charged on a subsequent disposal (provided the relief has not been withdrawn) only on the excess over original cost *before* allowing for BES relief. For shares issued after 18 March 1986, no capital gains tax is charged at all on the first disposal (provided again that the relief has not been withdrawn).

Where BES relief does not apply it may be possible to claim an alternative form of income tax relief (known as *venture capital relief*) on the cost of the investment where this subsequently becomes valueless.

8.1.3 Retirement benefits

The pension benefits that can be provided for directors under an Inland Revenue approved company pension scheme will usually far exceed those that can be obtained by self-employed individuals paying retirement annuity premiums as described in 5.1. The exact terms of these benefits will depend on the rules of the scheme but generally the main benefits that can be obtained are:

(1) A retirement pension of 2/3rds final salary for the director together with a widow's pension of 4/9ths final salary provided that there is at least 20 years' service with the company.
(2) Part of the pension in (1) may be commuted for a tax-free lump sum of up to 1½ times the director's final salary (subject to an upper limit of £150,000) provided that he has at least 20 years' service with the company.
(3) A lump sum of up to four times his salary together with a widow's pension of 4/9ths of final salary should the director die in the company's service before reaching retirement age. Arrangements can be made for any death in service benefit to be paid outside the director's estate and thereby be free of an inheritance tax charge.
(4) Annual increases related to the prevailing rate of increase in the retail prices index or any other suitable approved index up to a specified limit.

With effect from 4 January 1988 it will be possible for a director to set up a *personal pension scheme* along the lines described in 4.4.6.

8.1.4 Statutory requirements

A company is required to comply with a number of statutory provisions which inevitably increase its administration costs.

The most important of these are as follows:

(1) The accounts must be subject to annual audit by an independent qualified accountant who is required to report that the accounts show a 'true and fair view'.
(2) All shareholders are entitled to a copy of the audited accounts set out in the form laid down in the Companies Act. Small companies are allowed to use an abridged form of statutory accounts.
(3) A copy of the audited accounts must be filed with the Registrar of Companies and is then available for public inspection.
(4) Other information regarding the appointment or resignation of directors and how the company's shares are held also has to be filed with the Registrar.
(5) A company must keep formal minutes of directors' and shareholders' meetings.

8.2   THE TAXATION OF COMPANIES

8.2.1   The scheme of corporation tax

Companies are subject to corporation tax which is fixed by reference to the *financial year* running from 1 April to 31 March. Where the company's accounting period straddles 31 March so as to fall into two financial years, the taxable profits of the period have to be apportioned between the two years in order to determine the rates of tax applicable.

For the year ended 31 March 1988, the normal rate of

corporation tax has been fixed at 35% where the profits for the year exceed £500,000. Where the profits are less than £100,000, a lower rate (known as the *small companies rate*) of 27% applies, with marginal relief applicable between the limits of £100,000 and £500,000.

These limits of £100,000 and £500,000 are reduced where the accounting period is less than twelve months or where there are a number of companies in a group or otherwise under common control.

A company's profits are adjusted for corporation tax purposes in the same way as described for income tax in 1.6. One notable difference that arises because the company and its directors are separate persons is that directors' remuneration is normally allowable in full as a trading expense; directors are regarded as employees for tax purposes and their remuneration and any benefits in kind they receive from the company are taxed under Schedule E through the PAYE system.

Corporation tax is normally due and payable nine months after the end of the company's accounting period; for companies trading prior to 1965 when corporation tax was introduced a longer period of 'credit' for the payment of tax may apply though this is now being phased out.

8.2.2 Advance corporation tax

Where a company pays a dividend it has to pay tax at 27/73rds of the dividend to the Collector of Taxes. The advance corporation tax paid in this way can be deducted from the company's mainstream corporation tax liability but the amount that can be set off in any accounting period is limited to 27% of the company's taxable profits in that period; prior to 17 March 1987, ACT could not be set off against corporation tax on a company's capital gains (see 8.2.4). As far as a 'small company' as defined in 8.2.1 is concerned its mainstream corporation tax liability charged at a rate of 27% could be extinguished by the advance corporation tax paid.

ACT paid on a company's own dividend may exceed 27% of its taxable profits. Surplus ACT may be carried backwards for up to six years, starting with the last year first, or forwards indefinitely, or surrendered to a 51% subsidiary company. In the latter situation the ACT can be used to offset a current corporation tax liability or carried forward against future corporation tax liabilities. However, once surrendered it cannot be carried back.

ACT is payable fourteen days after the end of the quarter in which the dividend is paid. During the year, therefore, dividends should be paid at the beginning of the next quarter rather than at the end of the previous quarter. ACT paid in respect of dividends paid in the year is offset against corporation tax due for that year which is payable nine months after the year end or later. It follows, therefore, that dividends should be paid as near as possible to, but certainly before, the year end to enable offset against corporation tax to be taken as soon as possible thereafter.

Individual shareholders are treated as receiving a net dividend with an income tax credit equal to the ACT attributable to their dividend. It will be appreciated that the ACT rate is related to the basic rate of income tax; thus ACT at 27/73rds on the dividend paid is equivalent to 27% on the dividend plus the tax credit. Thus for the tax years up to 1985/86 when the basic rate was 30%, the corresponding rate of ACT was 3/7ths; for 1986/87 the basic rate was 29% and ACT was 29/71sts. This credit is available against any liability to higher rate tax that the shareholders may have; alternatively it may be repaid to them if they are not liable to tax on the dividend, e.g. because of unrelieved personal allowances.

The operation of this scheme is illustrated in the following example.

EXAMPLE 15

In the year ended 31 March 1988, Wiltshire Enterprises Ltd makes taxable profits of £600,000; on 31 July 1987 it paid a dividend of £73,000. Its tax position is as follows:

Profits chargeable to corporation tax	£600,000
Corporation tax at 35%	£210,000
Dividend paid	£73,000
ACT thereon at 27/73rds	£27,000
(=27% of £73,000 + £27,000)	

The company would actually account for its corporation tax liability in two parts:

	£
ACT due 14 October 1987	27,000
Mainstream corporation tax due 1 January 1989	183,000
	———
	£210,000

A shareholder who receives a dividend of £7,300 on this occasion is entitled to a tax credit of 27/73rds of this, i.e. £2,700. If his marginal rate of income tax on this income is 60%, he will have to pay further tax (known as *excess liability*) for the tax year 1987/88 of £3,300, arrived at as follows:

'Gross equivalent' of dividend	£10,000

	£
Income tax thereon at 60%	6,000
Less: Tax credit	2,700
Excess liability, normally due 1 December 1988	£3,300

8.2.3 Dividends received by a company

Dividends received from other UK companies are not liable to corporation tax in the hands of the recipient company. The tax credit attaching to dividends received from other UK companies can be used to *frank* a company's own dividends thus reducing the required payment of ACT. Consideration should therefore be given to investing surplus funds in shares of UK companies producing dividends so as to reduce any ACT payable. Where a company has current tax losses it may claim repayment of the tax credit attaching to those dividends by setting losses against the gross dividends. This can provide a cash flow advantage.

8.2.4 Capital gains of companies

A company's capital gains are now included with its profits and changed to corporation tax at the appropriate rate as described in 8.2.1. For disposals of assets made prior to 17 March 1987, capital gains were charged separately to corporation tax at an effective rate of 30%.

Capital losses may be set only against capital gains realized by the same company. Therefore, in a group situation assets on which gains are expected to arise should be transferred to a company with capital losses before any sale takes place; this inter-group transfer can be made free of tax with the transferee company 'inheriting' the transferor's acquisition cost. Care should be taken because in certain instances anti-avoidance legislation or the use by the Revenue of case law can negate the effectiveness of some transactions.

8.2.5   Double taxation of capital gains

It is possible on a winding up to incur a double tax charge. This arises because the company will pay corporation tax on its chargeable gains and individual shareholders may suffer a capital gains tax charge on any profit they realize when they receive their share of the liquidation proceeds. The introduction of the capital gains tax indexation allowance has gone some way to alleviating this disadvantage.

8.2.6   Close companies

A more stringent tax regime used to apply to *close companies*, broadly ones under the control of their directors or of five or fewer shareholders; these therefore included the large majority of privately owned family companies. Formerly there were strict requirements imposed on such companies as to the distribution of retained profits, but these have been largely repealed now as regards trading companies.

However one requirement has been retained. Where a close company makes a loan to a *participator*, broadly a shareholder, it is required to account for tax as if it were ACT at 27/73rds of the amount of the loan. When the loan is repaid, the corresponding tax can be recovered from the Revenue. This can clearly have adverse cash flow consequences.

Loans to *directors* in excess of £2,500 are prohibited under company law.

8.2.7.   Losses

Losses can be utilized against other income and gains in the year in which they are incurred or carried back to the previous year against all income and gains for that year or carried forward against future profits arising from the same trade, but *not* gains. Where tax losses arise from a claim for first-year allowances they can be carried back against all income and gains of the three preceding years starting with the last year first.

Where losses cannot be set off against other company income, there is no question of those losses being available for the personal benefit of the directors or shareholders.

8.2.8   Remuneration or dividends

It used to be best practice for an individual who was both a director and a shareholder in a company to draw remuneration from it rather than dividends. However recent changes in the tax system overall, notably the abolition of the investment income surcharge and the restructuring of national insurance contributions, indicate that a reconsideration of this approach may be appropriate.

Much depends on the particular circumstances of the company and the individuals concerned, and proper professional advice is essential. However here are some of the factors that should be borne in mind:

(1) An individual may claim personal allowances, etc. against dividend income as well as against remuneration.
(2) Pension scheme contributions may be paid only where there is a source of earned income, e.g. remuneration.
(3) National insurance contributions are not payable in respect of dividends: this can represent a substantial saving as compared with the Class 1 contributions due by both the individual and the company in respect of remuneration. On the other hand, there can be some loss of future benefit if contributions are not kept up.
(4) Remuneration is paid subject to PAYE. While this may take account of the individual's entitlement to allowances and deductions, it does mean that higher rate tax is being collected at the same time. Dividends are effectively paid out under deduction of basic rate at 27% only, leaving any higher rate tax to be collected later as explained in 8.2.2 and Example 15.
(5) Remuneration may be paid in arrears by way of a bonus, some time after the year end, when the company's results for the year are known, and related back so as to rank as a further deduction against that year's profits. Care needs to be taken to see that any amounts

that may have been drawn on account of such bonus payments are not treated as 'loans' so as to fall foul of the tax charge described in 8.2.6.

It is not possible to relate back a dividend payment in this way. As described in 8.2.2, the corresponding ACT must primarily be relieved against mainstream corporation tax on the profits of the accounting period in which the dividend is paid.

(6) PAYE tax and national insurance contributions have to be accounted for to the Revenue on a *monthly* basis. ACT has only to be accounted for *quarterly*.

(7) To avoid any challenge by the Revenue as to its allowability in the company's accounts, it is advisable to maintain directors' remuneration at a reasonable level consistent with the duties and responsibilities of the individuals concerned.

(8) The possible effect on the value of the company's shares may be important if a sale or other disposal is in view. The payment of remuneration obviously reduces the company's reported profits and will tend to depress the value of its shares; the payment of dividends on a regular basis may give the company a 'track record' so as to enhance that value.

Overall, whether individuals take their 'reward' by way of remuneration or dividend, it must be sensible to try to bring the rates of tax of the company and the individual into line as nearly as possible. It will be remembered that at present a company pays corporation tax at not more than 35%; an individual pays tax at 27% on taxable income up to £17,900, rising to 60% on the excess over £41,200 (at 1987/88 rates).

Where a company is making losses there may be little point in paying out remuneration, except to the extent necessary to cover the individuals' personal allowances. It should be noted that, in these circumstances, there may be restrictions under company law as to how much, if anything, may be paid out as dividends.

8.3 TRANSFER OF A BUSINESS TO A LIMITED COMPANY

8.3.1 Assessments on transferor business

The profits for the tax year in which the transferor business ceases are assessed on an actual basis. Also, the Inspector of Taxes has the right, as described in 6.3, to increase the assessments for the two immediately preceding years to the actual profits earned in those years. The Inspector will, of course, exercise this right only where this means that the assessable profits can be increased. This will usually apply where profits are rising in the closing years; and so, wherever possible, this should be avoided and incorporation, unless absolutely necessary for commercial reasons, should be deferred.

8.3.2 Valuation of trading stock

Where a business is transferred to a company in return for ordinary shares, trading stock should normally be valued at market value for income tax purposes. The reason for this is that the stock has been transferred for valuable consideration, i.e. shares issued by the company. Those shares will reflect the market value of the assets acquired by the company. However, provided the value of stock and work in progress is stated at the same value in the closing business as it is in the new company, the Revenue do not normally examine this closely. In the situation where stock has a market value appreciably in excess of its book value, care should be taken because this could result in the profits in the closing unincorporated business being much higher coupled with the possibility of making losses in the early years of the company's trade which might not be utilized very quickly.

8.3.3 Transfers of fixed assets

The market value of *plant and machinery* held in the unincorporated business and for which capital allowances have been claimed in the past is likely to exceed the balance of unallowed expenditure for tax purposes. Wherever possible, any substantial balancing charge should be avoided. It is possible for the previous business to agree to sell the plant and machinery to the company at its tax written-down value. Normally the Revenue are unable to substitute market value for the actual agreed consideration provided the company is able to claim capital allowances on its expenditure. Alternatively, it is possible for the plant and machinery to be transferred to the company at its open market value and a potential balancing charge avoided by submission of a joint election which has the following effect:

(1)   the original business is not treated as discontinued for capital allowance purposes; *and*

(2)   the company receives capital allowances in the future as if no sale or transfer had taken place.

This election is possible only where the company succeeds to the sole trader/partnership trade and the sole trader or partners and the company are connected persons. Such a claim must be made within six years of the change.

Where *industrial buildings* have been held by a sole trader or partnership and it is desired that they be transferred to the successor company, such buildings can be transferred into the company at a value equal to the unrelieved residue of expenditure available. If the property is retained by the original traders, stamp duty is saved and the potential danger of a double charge to capital gains tax is avoided on the liquidation of the company, but it can have adverse capital gains tax effects on other assets such as goodwill which are transferred to the company. However, any balancing charge which would arise on the footing that the building has been sold to the company at open market value can be avoided provided the company receives the benefit of future writing-down allowances and a suitable election to this effect is lodged.

For *agricultural buildings* acquired on or before 31 March 1986 the position is more straightforward: on transfer to the successor company the latter takes over the balance of allowances due for the remainder of the writing-down period. Where the expenditure on the buildings is incurred after 31 March 1986, there is a choice as to whether to follow the arrangement just mentioned or to treat the transfer as taking place at market value and recognize a balancing adjustment accordingly (see 3.5).

8.3.4 Losses

Where a business ceases it follows that unutilized losses can no longer be carried forward and relieved in the usual way against future profits. However, where a sole trader or partnership sells the business to a company, some relief is available provided the consideration is wholly or mainly shares in that company and the shares continue to be held throughout the year of assessment. In this situation losses can be carried forward and set off by the former owners against income received from the company. Losses are first set against remuneration and then against dividend income in any year until exhausted. This relief does not extend to excess capital allowances but in practice it should be possible to arrange matters so that none remain unutilized.

8.3.5 Capital gains tax

Where a business is transferred to a company there can be serious capital gains tax consequences. The transfer of a business to a company will usually involve the disposal of all or most of the assets employed in the business. Chargeable gains and perhaps allowable losses will therefore arise in respect of:

(1)   Goodwill.
(2)   Land and buildings.
(3)   Fixed plant and machinery.

(4) Investments.
(5) Business chattels with a market value in excess of £3,000.

Private motor cars are specifically excluded from a capital gains tax charge.

A charge to capital gains tax on the incorporation of a business can be deferred in whole or in part where the following conditions are met:

(1) all the assets of the business (other than cash) are transferred to the company; *and*
(2) the business is transferred as a going concern; *and*
(3) it is transferred wholly or partly in exchange for shares issued by the company.

It is important that in order that relief is obtained the whole of the assets of the business should be transferred. Omitting to transfer assets, other than cash, perhaps to save stamp duty, will negate any claim.

Provided the above conditions are satisfied, the chargeable gain is computed by calculating the total net gains arising on the disposal of the business assets and deducting a proportion of the net gains using the formula $(A \div B) \times$ net gain where A is the value of the shares obtained from the company and B is the total value of the consideration given by the company (which usually means shares and cash). The balance of any gains is assessed to capital gains tax.

EXAMPLE 16

David transfers his business into Wiltshire Enterprises Ltd in exchange for 20,000 ordinary shares valued at £100,000 and £10,000 cash. The assets transferred are as follows:

	Cost £	Market value £
Goodwill	Nil	20,000
Business premises	20,000	50,000
Plant and machinery	20,000	15,000
	40,000	85,000
Stock	15,000	20,000
Debtors	5,000	5,000
	£60,000	£110,000

The chargeable gain, ignoring indexation, arising is calculated as follows:

		£	£
Goodwill	value	20,000	
	cost	Nil	
			20,000
Business premises	value	50,000	
	cost	20,000	
			30,000

	£
Forward	50,000
Less amount rolled over	
$(100,000 \div 110,000) \times 50,000 =$	45,455
Gain now chargeable	£4,545

Where shares acquired in this way are subsequently disposed of, the amount rolled over, in the above example of £45,455, is deducted from the cost of the shares in computing any further chargeable gain.

EXAMPLE 17

David later sells his shares in Wiltshire Enterprises Ltd for £125,000:

	£	£
Sale proceeds		125,000
Less: Cost	100,000	
Less: Rolled over	45,455	
		54,545
Chargeable gain		£70,455

Where a number of different classes of shares are issued on an incorporation the sum rolled over is apportioned according to the market value of each class of share at the time of the exchange.

For ease indexation allowance has not been taken into account in the above calculations. However, an indexation allowance will commence to accrue from the date on which the business was transferred in exchange for shares.

The arrangement described above does suffer from one disadvantage. It may be preferred that a material part of the consideration for the transfer should be in cash or its equivalent; it follows that a corresponding proportion of the overall gain is immediately chargeable to capital gains tax. This could be particularly expensive where the non-share element was in the form of a loan to be paid off as the company's cash flow permitted; this would still be regarded as the equivalent of cash, so giving rise to a liability to tax without the cash to pay it having been received.

One way of dealing with this situation would be to structure such a loan as loan stock. The gain attributable to this part of the consideration could still be rolled over until such time as it, or any part of it, was repaid.

Another solution would be for the proprietors to make a gift to the company of those assets showing substantial latent capital gain, so that the shares/cash/loan consideration would be largely or wholly applied to assets which are not subject to capital gains tax at all or which only carry a small potential gain. A correspondingly small proportion of that gain would then become chargeable, while the gain on the gifted assets could be held over by a joint election of the donors and the company.

To avoid any problems arising in relation to inheritance tax, the shareholders in the successor company should hold shares in the same proportions as their interests in the predecessor business.

EXAMPLE 18

Taking the figures for assets in Example 16, if the consideration of £110,000 is to be settled as to 20,000 shares valued at £70,000 and cash of £40,000, the chargeable gain would be dealt with as follows:

	£
Amount rolled over	
$(70,000 \div 110,000) \times 50,000 =$	31,818
Balance now chargeable	18,182
	£50,000

If, however, the goodwill and the business assets were gifted to the company and the remaining assets were sold in consideration of 20,000 shares at par and cash of £20,000, the potential gain of £50,000 on those assets could be held over; in effect the company would be treated as acquiring the assets at their original cost of nil and £20,000 respectively. The company's liability to tax on their eventual disposal would be correspondingly greater but on the other hand the company might be able to take advantage of rollover relief on the acquisition of replacement assets as described in 4.3. The shares and cash would wholly relate to assets on which no gain arose and there would therefore be nothing to roll over.

If it is decided that it would be better to retain the business premises in an individual's ownership and not pass it into the company and yet not lose the benefit of rolling over the capital gains tax liability on an incorporation, it will be necessary to convert it into a non-business asset. This might be done by gifting the property to the trader's spouse and leasing the property back. Any adjustments necessary to the business's balance sheet could be done via the proprietor's capital account. The asset which would then be transferred into the company would be the leasehold interest. Professional advice should be taken to ensure that all the terms under which a transaction takes place are commercial and it may be advisable to carry out such an operation well before incorporation.

8.3.6   Value added tax

Where a business is disposed of as a going concern for VAT purposes, this is a supply made in the course or furtherance of the business and VAT is chargeable on the sale of fixtures, fittings, plant and machinery, stock and goodwill. However, no taxable supply is deemed to have been made, and consequently VAT will not be charged, where the business is incorporated and the following conditions are satisfied:

(1)   the transferee uses the assets transferred to carry on the same kind of business as that carried on by the transferor; *and*
(2)   where only part of an existing business is acquired that part must be capable of separate operation; *and*
(3)   the transferee must be a taxable person, or become one at the time of the transfer, if the transferor was a taxable person.

Only on very rare occasions should a bona fide incorporation of a business find itself liable to VAT on that event.

In this situation it is possible for both the transferor and the transferee to apply for the transferee to take over the transferor's original VAT registration number provided that from the date of the transfer the original business's registration is cancelled and the new business, not previously registered, is liable to be so registered. The net effect is that the company stands in the shoes of the sole trader/partnership taking over both its VAT rights and obligations. The company would thus become liable to submit any outstanding returns and to pay any VAT due.

8.3.7 Stamp duty

This is a duty on certain documents. If property is capable of being transferred in a way avoiding the use of a document no stamp duty will be payable. However, duty will normally be payable at a rate of 1% on the value of the consideration for the conveyance or transfer on a sale of land and buildings, goodwill, fixed plant and machinery, fixtures and fittings, debtors, shares, etc. and bank deposit accounts, but not bank current accounts. There are occasions where matters can be arranged so that stamp duty is mitigated or avoided altogether but care should be taken as the rollover relief on incorporation mentioned above may be jeopardized. As a general rule it will be difficult to avoid stamp duty on the transfer of land, goodwill and debtors but it is possible in respect of plant, trading stock and cash.

8.3.8 Capital duty

This is payable at the rate of 1% on the greater of the nominal value of the shares issued or allotted by a limited company and the value of the assets contributed less liabilities assumed or discharged. It applies on the initial issue of shares or on an increase in the share capital represented by the contribution of assets of any kind.

8.3.9 Employees

Where an unincorporated business ceases and its trade is passed to a company, technically all the employees become redundant; however, provided they are given proper notice and employment on identical terms and conditions is offered by the company the liability to make redundancy payments is avoided. Essentially, the company steps into the shoes of the transferor business and takes over all past and future employee liabilities. As far as the employees are concerned their employment by the unincorporated business and the company will count as one continuous employment for the purposes of the employee protection legislation.

8.4 INHERITANCE TAX

8.4.1 General principles

Inheritance tax was introduced in the Budget of 18 March 1986 to replace the previous capital transfer tax; the detailed provisions are contained in the 1986 and 1987 Finance Acts. The notes which follow look at the operation and planning implications of the new tax; readers who are concerned about their position in relation to transactions that took place prior to 18 March 1986 should seek professional advice as a matter of urgency.

The new scheme applies generally to tax the aggregate value of assets passing on *death* and by *gifts made within seven years before death* where this exceeds £90,000; the latter are included with the assets passing at death at their value at the date of the gift, but using the rates of tax in force at the date of death. However, only gifts made up to *three years* before death are subject to tax in full; for gifts made more than three years but less than seven years before death a form of tapering relief applies so that only a proportion of the full charge applies.

Details of the rates of tax and of the tapering relief are given in Appendix D.

Apart from the 'seven-year rule' already described, the tax does not generally apply to lifetime gifts made between individuals and into certain 'qualifying' trusts (see 8.5): such gifts are called *potentially exempt transfers* ('PETs'). However, it does apply at half the normal rates to transfers of assets made into discretionary trusts.

One important exception to the above relates to *gifts with reservation*, i.e. those which are not made free and unencumbered but where the donor continues to enjoy some benefit from the gifted asset. An example of this would be the gift of a house to a member of the donor's family that is subject to him (the donor) continuing to live in it rent-free. In this situation the gift is treated as made only when the reservation is released or the benefit comes to an end; in the example given this could apply when the donor moves out to live elsewhere, giving up his rights of occupation, or perhaps on his death. If the gift is thereby treated as taking place on the donor's death or within a period of seven years before, inheritance tax will apply.

There are also a number of exemptions available to reduce the potential exposure to inheritance tax on lifetime gifts. The most notable of these are:

- Exemption for gifts between husband and wife (this also applies to assets passing to the surviving spouse on death).
- Annual exemption of £3,000 per donor.
- Small gifts exemption of £250 per donee.
- Exemption for normal expenditure out of income and for family maintenance.
- Exemption for certain wedding gifts.
- Exemption for gifts to charities, political parties and certain public bodies concerned with the national heritage (this also applies, with certain exceptions, on death).

Note that, unlike income tax and capital gains tax, husband and wife are treated as separate persons for inheritance tax.

There is also no general exemption for an individual's principal private residence.

Although the general exclusion from tax of lifetime gifts between individuals has in many cases reduced the obvious immediacy of estate planning in an individual's lifetime it must still be vital to keep matters under continuing review, particularly where the prospective donor is more elderly so that the possibility of the seven-year charge applying cannot be excluded. The particular benefits of planning during the early phase of a company's development are:

(1) The future growth in value of shares in the company which are transferred will arise in the donee's ownership and therefore outside the donor's estate;

(2) It may be possible to agree a favourable valuation of the shares where the company's trade is not fully established (see 8.4.2).

8.4.2 Valuation of shares

Companies offer greater opportunities for tax planning than partnerships. This is because the ownership of a company can be more easily fragmented into smaller units than can a partnership and those units are more easily transferred.

Although shares in an unquoted private company, typical of the sort of entity now being considered, do not have a market value in the normal sense that this is understood, a series of guidelines and rules have been developed through the courts over the years to enable a basis of valuation to be applied in these circumstances. It is outside the scope of this book to look at this area in detail, but it is worth mentioning the fundamental principle that shares representing a majority holding (over 50%), or a part of a majority holding, are normally valued by reference to the underlying assets of the company, and so may reflect a materially higher value than a minority holding (less than 50%), where the normal base is the company's earnings, or, in the case of a small minority holding (less than 10%), the company's dividend record.

It should also be noted that valuations for inheritance tax purposes are based on the 'loss to donor' principle, so that the amount transferred is found by comparing the value of the donor's holding before and after the transfer. This can lead to wide variations in valuation for inheritance tax purposes, depending on whether the donor's holding at the material times is large or small. It should be noted here that this concept does *not* apply in relation to valuations for capital gains tax or stamp duty purposes, where it is the size of the holding being transferred that is critical.

This is a complex area and professional advice should always be sought where any transfers of shares in an unquoted company are contemplated.

8.4.3   Business property relief

Where a business is incorporated there can be an adverse effect on the *business property relief* available to the former proprietors, and the following points should be remembered:

(1)   Where an individual has a controlling shareholding in a company he should continue to qualify for 50% business property relief. To do this it is necessary that the interest in the company should be a controlling one and that all the shares are owned for a minimum of two years. For this purpose the period of ownership or interest in the original business can be taken into account.

(2)   Prior to 17 March 1987, the relief on minority shareholdings in unquoted companies was limited to 30%. For transfers made on or after that date, the relief on shareholdings of more than 25% is increased to 50%, provided that the transferor had held over 25% in the company for a minimum of two years. Where this test

is not satisfied and for shareholdings of 25% or less, the relief remains at 30%.

(3) Whereas all partners in a business can qualify for 50% business property relief, should they become minority shareholders in an unquoted company this relief may be reduced to 30%.

(4) Where a *controlling* shareholder allows the company to use land, buildings, machinery and plant owned by him or her in its business, he or she will normally qualify for 30% business property relief on the value of those assets. Note that this relief is not available at all to a *minority* shareholder.

Where a lifetime gift is made which then meets the tests of business property relief, the relief is given only if the tests are also satisfied at the date of the donor's death.

At first sight it would seem that as regards the relative relief on their shareholdings, controlling shareholders have a distinct advantage over minority shareholders. However it must be remembered that the latter's shares are likely to be valued at a materially lower level than the former's. In practice, the net chargeable value per share is often not significantly different.

8.5 THE USE OF SETTLEMENTS

Settlements can be a powerful tool in the field of longer-term tax planning. What follows can be only a brief summary and specialist professional advice should always be taken.

It is always important to have regard first and foremost

to the commercial considerations before looking at the tax opportunities, but subject to that the latter can be considerable.

As mentioned in 8.4.1, gifts into certain trusts qualify as potentially exempt transfers in the same way as gifts between individuals, i.e. a charge to inheritance tax arises only if the transferor dies within seven years of making the gift. The trusts which are treated in this way are accumulation and maintenance settlements (see 8.5.3), trusts for the disabled and (with effect from 17 March 1987) interest in possession settlements (see 8.5.4).

It is worth mentioning that individual shareholders setting up a settlement can, if they so wish, be appointed the first named trustee which gives them control over the voting power of the shares and in practical terms puts them in the same position in relation to the company as they were before. It is usual to appoint at least one other trustee who could be a professional adviser.

It is also possible for a settlor to be a beneficiary of his settlement, but this would fall foul of the provisions relating to gifts with reservation mentioned in 8.4.1, so that any inheritance tax advantage would be negated; this problem can be avoided if the settlor excludes himself from benefit more than seven years before his death.

8.5.1   The discretionary settlement

This gives the trustees power to distribute capital and income among a class of beneficiaries at their discretion, rather than on any fixed basis; alternatively the trustees can accumulate income.

The class of beneficiaries could include the share-holder/settlor's spouse, children and grandchildren and other relatives or persons (such as charities) and there could be power to add or exclude beneficiaries in the future.

The transfer of funds into the settlement is a transfer for *inheritance tax* purposes and in principle will attract tax at half the rates set out in Appendix D. However with the use of business property relief and the various exemptions, it is possible to transfer a substantial amount without incurring any liability to tax.

EXAMPLE 19

David transfers in 1987/88 his 60% shareholding in Wiltshire Enterprises Ltd, valued at £192,000, to a discretionary trust he has set up.

	£
Value of shares	192,000
Business property relief at 50%	96,000
	96,000
Annual exemptions for two years	6,000
	£90,000

If David has made no transfers of value for inheritance tax purposes in the past seven years, this amount will be within the nil rate band in the inheritance tax table reproduced at Appendix D, so that no tax is chargeable.

If the transfer does give rise to a charge to tax, this, if it is paid by the trustees, can usually be paid by ten interest-free annual instalments; this relief applies to most categories of assets which cannot readily be disposed of, for example unquoted shares. In turn this tax could be funded by the settlor making an annual gift to the trustees: if this is within his £3,000 annual exemption, there will still be no tax to pay.

There is a charge to inheritance tax on each tenth anniversary of the settlement. This is calculated on the value of the assets in the settlement and is charged at 15% of the normal rates. The maximum rate of tax payable in these circumstances is therefore 15% of 60%, i.e. 9%. If a number of settlements are set up, the value of each one is looked at separately for these purposes, so it may be possible to reduce or eliminate the charge that would otherwise arise on a single settlement provided sufficient care is taken in their creation.

When a distribution takes place prior to the tenth anniversary, the effective rate of inheritance tax payable by the trust is found by applying the lifetime rates then in force to the value of the assets when they entered the settlement (but ignoring for this purpose any business property relief). If this notional rate is nil, then this still applies, even though the value at the distribution may be considerably greater than that originally put into the settlement.

So far as *capital gains tax* is concerned, this also applies on the transfer of assets to the settlement but any liability can be held over in accordance with the usual rules relating to gifts. Where a sale of shares is anticipated (and this could be particularly important in the case of a flotation on The Stock Exchange or the Unlisted Securities Market) it may be

possible to defer payment indefinitely of any charge to CGT
by appointing non-resident trustees to the settlement. This
will crystallize any earlier held-over gain, but this may be a
small price to pay as the gains realized by the non-resident
trustees will generally become chargeable in the UK only
when the settlor or a member of his family receives capital
from the settlement. Where the ultimate beneficiary is not
UK domiciled and neither resident nor ordinarily resident
in the UK this deferral may become permanent.

Where the settlor and/or his spouse are included in the
class of beneficiaries, the income of such a settlement is
treated as their income for *income tax* purposes, irrespective
of whether it is paid to them. Otherwise the income is
subject to a special rate of tax at present fixed at 45%.

Under the Finance Act 1985, *stamp duty* on gifts was
abolished with effect from 26 March 1985. Therefore no duty
is payable on assets transferred to a settlement.

8.5.2   The personal settlement

Under this disposition, the income of the settlement would
usually be payable to the settlor for life, then to his widow
for life and thereafter to their children and/or other beneficiaries on fixed or discretionary trusts. The trustees could
have power to pay capital to the settlor or his spouse/widow
at any time.

In this situation, no *inheritance tax* would be payable on
the transfer of assets into the settlement as their underlying
value continues to be treated as part of the settlor's estate
for tax purposes. Tax may arise subsequently, e.g. on the

death of the settlor or of his widow, in accordance with the normal rules.

The same *capital gains tax* and *stamp duty* consequences arise as described for discretionary settlements in 8.5.1.

Income tax continues to be charged on the income arising on the settlor in his lifetime and on his widow during her lifetime.

8.5.3   The accumulation and maintenance settlement

This is a particular form of *discretionary settlement* which carries some peculiar advantages of its own.

It is a settlement which does not include the settlor or his spouse as a beneficiary but instead concentrates on their children as the primary beneficiaries; an essential condition is that a child of the settlor must at least become entitled to receive *income* from the settlement at an age no greater than twenty-five. *Capital* can pass to the child at any time and it is usual to leave this aspect to the trustees' discretion.

While *inheritance tax* may be potentially payable on the transfer into the settlement if the settlor dies within seven years, no further liability to the tax can arise either within the settlement or on the eventual transfer to a beneficiary. It may however be payable on the death of a beneficiary who has obtained an interest in the income but not in the capital.

The *capital gains tax* and *stamp duty* consequences are as described in 8.5.1, while *income tax* is charged only at the special rate of 45% until a beneficiary becomes entitled to the income or a share of it. If income is received by a minor beneficiary who is a child of the settler a tax charge will arise to the parent.

8.5.4   The interest in possession settlement

This type of settlement provides that while the capital is to be held by trustees, named beneficiaries are to have an immediate entitlement to income. The capital may pass to those beneficiaries at some later date or be disposed of in other ways on their deaths. It should not include the settlor or his spouse as a beneficiary as this would negate the tax advantages.

Where a transfer into such a settlement is made on or after 17 March 1987, no *inheritance tax* is payable unless the transferor dies within seven years. Similarly no immediate charge to the tax arises where a beneficiary's interest comes to an end (thought it remains potentially chargeable for seven years) if in that event one of the following situations applies:

(1)   Another individual obtains an interest in the trust, either in the capital or the income;
(2)   The trust assets pass to an accumulation and maintenance settlement (see 8.5.3) or to a trust for the disabled;
(3)   The value of another individual's estate is increased.

For transfers made before 17 March 1987, this relief did not apply and the position was as described for discretionary settlements in 8.5.1.

Otherwise the assets of the trust are treated as part of the estate of a beneficiary entitled to income from it for the purpose of determining the inheritance tax payable on his death.

The *capital gains tax* and *stamp duty* consequences are as set out in 8.5.1.

As the income is payable to beneficiaries as of right, they are chargeable to *income tax* on it as part of their total income. Exceptionally, if a beneficiary is a minor child of the settlor, the income is assessed on him as the child's parent.

While such a settlement may include beneficiaries of any age, it is particularly suitable where children over the age of twenty-five are involved so that an accumulation and maintenance settlement (see 8.5.3) cannot be used.

8.6   USE OF LIFE INSURANCE

A method of funding a potential inheritance tax liability on a significant holding of shares in the company is to take out a joint life and survivor policy on the lives of the shareholder and his spouse so that on the death of the survivor, and especially where assets are passed to the spouse on the first death, the policy proceeds will be payable to the donees to enable them to meet the capital transfer tax liability. This preserves the assets of the estate including the shares in the family company. Such policies can be written in trust for the benefit of the donees so as not to be included in the estates of the individual or his spouse.

Whether the premiums payable are considered to be commercially acceptable depends upon the individual facts.

It would be necessary to have regard to the age and the health of the individual who it is proposed will be insured and the premiums required by the insurer together with the amount of tax that needs to be covered.

Where the proprietor is in very poor health and thereby uninsurable and little or no pension arrangements have been made, consideration should be given to setting up a personal pension fund with a substantial contribution from the company. In the event of the early death of the proprietor the bulk, if not all, of the pension fund could provide a death in service benefit payable free of inheritance tax at the trustees' discretion.

8.7   GETTING CASH OUT

In 8.2.8 consideration was given to the relative merits of taking income out of the company in the form of remuneration or as dividends. In the long term, more significant problems can emerge where a shareholder wishes to realize his or her *capital* in the company in a tax-efficient fashion. This is not necessarily straightforward or easy in the case of an unquoted, closely held private company with no, or at least no obvious, market for its shares.

In addressing the challenge, a great deal depends on the financial position of the company on the one hand and of the major shareholders and their families on the other; the interests of outside shareholders, for example those who have invested money in the company within the terms of the business expansion scheme and are therefore locked into the company for at least five years (see 8.1.2), must not be disregarded.

These are some of the questions which major shareholders need to ask themselves if they are looking for a way through this problem:

- Do I wish to realize my shareholding in full and get out of the company?
- Would I like to realize a substantial part of my capital which is locked up in the company, but without giving up voting control and the privileges (as well as the responsibilities) that go with it?
- Do I want my interest in the company to be preserved for the benefit of my family?
- Would I prefer to continue to be involved in running one part of the company's operations and enter into a deal whereby other members of the family, or other outside interests, take over the rest of the company's undertaking?

Here are some of the ways in which answers to these questions may be found:

(1) *Full Stock Exchange Listing*. This is only for substantial companies, say with a market valuation in excess of £2mn, and in practice is unlikely to be the chosen direct route for a private company.
(2) *Unlisted Securities Market quotation*. This is less complex and correspondingly less expensive than (1), but does allow a market to be initiated in the company's shares without the founding shareholders losing effective control.

(3) *The Third Market*. This was started by The Stock Exchange in January 1987 with the intention of extending the possibility of raising outside capital to a larger number of young and growing companies for whom (1) or (2) is not a suitable route. It requires a minimum amount of regulation, delegating most of this to the stockbrokers concerned.

(4) *Over-the-counter market*. This is an altogether more informal market than those described in (1), (2) and (3). It is operated by a number of licensed dealers with no specific regulatory requirements.

(5) *Sale to institutional investors*. It is possible to sell off a substantial part of the company's equity to institutional investors by the issue and placing of non-voting shares so that voting control still remains with the founding shareholders.

(6) *Reconstruction or demerger*. Procedures are available within the tax system whereby, subject to certain conditions, it is possible to separate various parts of a company or group so that ownership of those parts passes to different shareholders.

(7) *Purchase by a company of its own shares*. Where it is not feasible or desirable to sell off part of the company's shares to outside investors, it may be possible to take advantage of the provisions which enable a company to buy its own shares from shareholders in part or in full. There are various conditions that have to be satisfied, but this can be an attractive way for individual shareholders who want to realize their investment.

Clearly the importance of obtaining experienced professional advice in this area cannot be over-emphasized.

APPENDIX A.   INCOME TAX RATES AND ALLOWANCES 1987/88

Rates of income tax

Rate %	Band of taxable income £	Cumulative tax £
27	1–17,900	4,833
40	17,901–20,400	5,833
45	20,401–25,400	8,083
50	25,401–33,300	12,033
55	33,301–41,200	16,378
60	over 41,200	—

Personal allowances

	£
Single person's allowance	2,425
Wife's earned income allowance (maximum)	2,425
Married man's allowance	3,795
Dependent relative – male claimant	100
– 'single' female claimant	145
Daughter's or son's services	55
Blind person's relief	540
Additional personal allowance ('single parent' families)	1,370
Widow's bereavement allowance	1,370

Single person's age allowance		
65–80:	2,960	Income
Over 80:	3,070	limit
Married man's age allowance		£9,800
65–80:	4,675	
over 80:	4,845	
Life assurance premiums paid on policies in force on 13 March 1984	15% deduction from total premiums paid	

Note

Detailed rules as to the entitlement to any of these allowances will need to be checked in individual cases.

APPENDIX B. CORPORATION TAX RATES 1987 AND 1988

	Year ended 31 March	
	1987	1988
Normal rate	35%	35%
Small companies rate (see note 1)	29%	27%
Marginal rate (see note 2)	36·5%	37%
Chargeable gains effective rate (see note 3)	30%	35%/27%

Notes

1 Applicable to total profits up to £100,000.
2 Applicable to total profits between £100,000 and £500,000.
3 For disposals on or after *17 March 1987*, companies pay corporation tax on their chargeable gains at the normal rate or small companies rate as applicable.

APPENDIX C.   NATIONAL INSURANCE CONTRIBUTIONS 1987/88

CLASS 1 EMPLOYED

	Employees	*Employers*
Not contracted out		
– *on all earnings*		
up to £38·99 per week	nil	nil
up to £64·99 per week	5·00%	5·00%
up to £99·99 per week	7·00%	7·00%
up to £149·99 per week	9·00%	9·00%
up to £295 per week	9·00%	10·45%
on excess over £295 per week	nil	10·45%
Contracted out – *on all earnings* up		
to £38·99 per week	nil	nil
up to £64·99 per week		
on first £39	5·00%	5·00%
on balance	2·85%	0·90%
up to £99·99 per week		
on first £39	7·00%	7·00%
on balance	4·85%	2·90%
up to £149·99 per week		
on first £39	9·00%	9·00%
on balance	6·85%	4·90%
up to £295 per week		
on first £39	9·00%	10·45%
on balance	6·85%	6·35%
on excess over £295 per week	nil	10·45%

CLASSES 2 and 4 SELF-EMPLOYED

	Employees	Employers
	nil	nil
Class 2 fixed per week		£3·85
no liability if earning below £2,125 per year		
Class 4 earnings related		6·3%*
on profits between £4,590 and £15,340 a year		

CLASS 3 NON-EMPLOYED

Voluntary rate per week	£3·75

*Half these contributions rank for income tax relief.

APPENDIX D.   CAPITAL TAXES 1987/88

Inheritance tax (effective from 17 March 1987)

Lower limit	Upper limit	Rate of tax	Tax to top of band
£	£	%	£
Nil	90,000	Nil	Nil
90,000	140,000	30	15,000
140,000	220,000	40	47,000
220,000	330,000	50	102,000
330,000	—	60	—

These rates also apply to chargeable lifetime transfers made within the three-year period prior to the date of death.

For lifetime transfers made more than three years but less than seven years before death, only a proportion of the full charge is applicable, as follows:

Years between transfer and death	Proportion of full charge
	%
3–4	80
4–5	60
5–6	40
6–7	20

Capital gains tax (effective from 6 April 1987)

Annual exemptions	
individuals	£6,600
trusts	£3,300
Rate of tax	30%

APPENDIX E.   TRADING EXPENSES –
TAX-DEDUCTIBLE ITEMS

The expenses below are allowable in calculating business profits to the extent that they are incurred wholly and exclusively for business purposes (the list is not exhaustive).

- A proportion of premiums on leases to the extent that these are chargeable in the hands of the recipient, spread over the term of the lease.
- Accountants' fees.
- Advertising.
- Bad debts, in the year written off or incurred.
- Bank charges – business.
- Debt collection.
- Entertainment expenses of overseas customers and staff within reason.
- Expenses of business premises including rent and rates, light and heat, repairs, insurance and cleaning, printing, postage, stationery, telephone.
- Expenses of use of home as office – in particular cleaning, heat and light, telephone (ensure no part used exclusively or there can be adverse capital gains tax consequences).
- General operating expenses.
- Gifts which are an advertisement for the business provided that the value does not exceed £10 for each recipient in each year: the gifts must incorporate a conspicuous advertisement for the donor and must not

consist of food, drink, tobacco or a token exchangeable for goods.
- Goods bought for resale.
- Hire charges.
- Incidental costs of obtaining loan finance.
- Interest payments.
- Legal and professional charges of a revenue nature, e.g. preparation of trading contracts and settling of trading disputes.
- Materials consumed in manufacturing processes.
- Motor expenses including: licence, insurance, parking fees (but not fines), petrol, oil, maintenance and repairs.
- Pension scheme contributions.
- Pensions paid to past employees and their dependants.
- Plant hire.
- Pre-trading expenditure up to three years before trading commences.
- Rates.
- Redundancy payments to employees.
- Salary and wages costs of employees only.
- Secretarial and book-keeping expenses.
- Staff welfare.
- Subscriptions to trade, business or professional associations.
- Travel expenses.
- Uniforms or protective clothing for employees.
- VAT on purchases and expenses where not registered for VAT or partly exempt.

APPENDIX F.   TRADING EXPENSES – NON-ALLOWABLE ITEMS

Any payment, or parts thereof, of expenses not wholly or exclusively laid out for the purposes of the business are not deductible in calculating business profits. These include:

- Capital improvements.
- Charges on income, e.g. annuities paid to former partners.
- Charitable donations unless wholly for business purposes.
- Clothes for work.
- Drawings.
- Entertaining expenses of UK customers.
- Excessive remuneration, particularly to relatives or connected persons.
- General reserves made for anticipated expenses such as repairs or bad debts, i.e. where they are not specific.
- Legal and professional fees of a capital nature, e.g. property purchase.
- Non-business element of expenses.
- Parking fines or any breaches of the law in general.
- Payments, or interest on delayed payment, of taxes.
- Personal expenses.
- Political donations.
- Taxation advice.
- Travel expenses of wife accompanying husband on business trip or vice versa unless purely commercial.

APPENDIX G. CAPITAL ALLOWANCES – PLANT AND MACHINERY

- Advertising boards and screens.
- Aerials.
- Air conditioning and ventilation equipment together with associated installation costs and professional fees.
- Alarms.
- Alterations to buildings.
- Architects' and other professional fees relating to items of plant.
- Baths.
- Blinds.
- Boilers.
- Burglar alarms and other security equipment including cameras, screens, fencing and barriers.
- Canteen equipment and fittings.
- Carpets and other removable floor coverings.
- Cash registers.
- Clocks (including wiring).
- Computers.
- Cooking equipment.
- Counters and fittings in shops.
- Curtains.
- Demountable partitions, provided that these are in fact moved from time to time.
- Dispensers and rails.
- Display lighting and associated electrical work.
- Door closers.

- Double glazing (for use in connection with air conditioning).
- Ducting for ventilation and heating systems.
- Electrical switchgear, controls, motors.
- Electrical wiring closely related to accepted items of plant.
- Electrically operated roller shutters and doors.
- Elevators.
- Emergency lighting.
- Escalators and travelators including installation costs.
- False ceilings where the ceiling forms an integral part of the air conditioning system.
- Fans.
- Fire alarms.
- Fire protection equipment.
- Fire safety expenditure carried out to comply with instructions from the fire authority.
- Furniture.
- Generators.
- Grain silos.
- Gymnasium equipment.
- Hand driers.
- Heating installations, fittings, etc.
- Hoists.
- Hoses.
- Hot water plumbing.
- Incinerators.
- Insulation to an existing industrial building.
- Internal telephone systems.
- Kitchen equipment.
- Laundry equipment.

- Lavatories, washbasins, sanitary fittings.
- Letterboxes.
- Lifts and lift indicators including lift shafts, motor rooms.
- Light fittings designed to create atmosphere or ambience or for a special purpose, e.g. shop window lighting.
- Lightning conductors.
- Lockers, mirrors and cloakroom equipment.
- Loose floor coverings and door mats.
- Mirrors.
- Murals in hotels.
- Personal and public address systems.
- Piped music fittings.
- Pumps.
- Racking and shelving including removable cupboards.
- Radiators.
- Refrigeration units.
- Refuse collection and disposal systems.
- Safes and strongrooms.
- Safety equipment, screens.
- Screens for window displays (movable).
- Security devices.
- Showers.
- Smoke detectors.
- Special housing for plant.
- Staff lockers.
- Storage tanks.
- Strengthened floors.
- Swimming pools in hotels.
- Switchboards and switchgear.
- Tapestries in pubs and hotels.

- Telephones.
- Teleprinters and telex machines.
- Televisions.
- Telex equipment, conduits, etc.
- Transformers.
- Tube conveyor systems and other types of document conveyors.
- Video equipment.
- Water treatment and filtration.
- Weighbridge.
- Welfare equipment.
- Window panels, lighting, sockets, etc. for shop front.